The Elements of STRATEGY

A pocket guide to the essence of successful business strategy

Mark Daniell

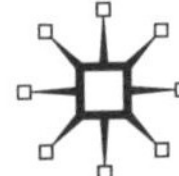

First published in 2006 by
PALGRAVE MACMILLAN
Houndmills, Basingstoke, Hampshire RG21 6XS and
175 Fifth Avenue, New York, N.Y. 10010
Companies and representatives throughout the world.

PALGRAVE MACMILLAN is the global academic imprint of the Palgrave Macmillan division of St. Martin's Press, LLC and of Palgrave Macmillan Ltd. Macmillan® is a registered trademark in the United States, United Kingdom and other countries. Palgrave is a registered trademark in the European Union and other countries.

ISBN-13: 978–0–230–00906–6
ISBN-10: 0–230–00906–9

This book is printed on paper suitable for recycling and made from fully managed and sustained forest sources.

A catalogue record for this book is available from the British Library.

A catalog record for this book is available from The Library of Congress.

10 9 8 7 6 5 4 3 2
15 14 13 12 11 10 09 08 07 06

Typeset by Exeter Premedia Services, Chennai

Printed and bound in China

Table of Contents

Acknowledgements vii

Introduction: The Value of Strategy 1

Part I. History and Overview 3

I.I Lessons from the Past 3

Element 1: Missing Elements of Traditional Strategy 3
Element 2: Traditional Models of Strategy 7
Element 3: The 7S's Model 14
Element 4: Sources of Insight 16

I.II Phases of Strategy 20

Element 5: Respecting Process Principles 20
Element 6: Diagnostic Phase 24
Element 7: Design Phase 28
Element 8: Implementation Phase 32
Element 9: Documenting Strategy 36

I.III Lessons for the Future 38

Element 10: Differentiating Characteristics 38
Element 11: Improving Creativity 42
Element 12: Managing Trends and Influences 46
Element 13: The 7C's Model + Results 51
Element 14: The "Rights" of Strategy 53

Part II. Principles of the New Paradigm 55

II.I Sharpening Your Focus 55

Element 15: Comparative Option Valuation 55
Element 16: Setting Priorities 58
Element 17: SMARTER Goals 61
Element 18: Tactics 63

II.II Responsibility and Engagement 66

Element 19: Corporate Responsibility 66
Element 20: Why Become Engaged? 70
Element 21: How the Private Sector Can Contribute 74
Element 22: A Practical Approach 77

II.III Leadership and Organization 81

Element 23: Principles of Leadership 81
Element 24: Strategic Organization 85
Element 25: Trends in Organizational Design 88
Element 26: Principles of the Orpheus Process 91
Element 27: Testing Organizational Design 94

The Final Element: Beginning Your Own Strategy 97

Epilogue 101

Acknowledgements

In creating this distilled version of my book ***STRATEGY: A step-by-step approach to the development and presentation of world class business strategy*** (Palgrave Macmillan, 2004), I am indebted to all those who contributed to that larger work.

In addition to echoing my thanks to the individuals and organizations contributing to the original edition of ***STRATEGY***, I would like to thank Hilary Galea, whose editing efforts, attention to detail and unstinting support led to a final result which is far better than anything I could have accomplished on my own.

I would be remiss if I did not note the obvious influence of the two authors of *The Elements of Style*, William Strunk Jr. and E.B. White. Their efforts served as both a model and an inspiration for this work.

Finally, I would like to acknowledge and thank my parents, Samuel and Zandra Daniell, for more than a half century of love and support.

This book is dedicated to them.

Introduction: The Value of Strategy

What is strategy?

Why is strategy so valuable? And how can we, as employees, managers or owners of businesses, be sure that our strategies are as effective as possible?

This book answers these questions—and many more—posed by those wishing to make a positive contribution to the future of their own businesses.

Let's start with a definition of strategy.

Having spent over twenty years in one of the world's leading strategic consulting firms, and benefiting from additional experience as a director of an international investment bank, as a start-up entrepreneur and as president of a publicly listed company, the most useful definition of business strategy I have found so far is quite simple:

> *Strategy is the art and science of informed action to achieve a specific vision, an overarching objective, or a higher purpose for a business enterprise.*

Strategy embraces many disciplines and areas of business activity: competition, human resources, technology, organization, leadership, communication, implementation and inspiration.

Together, the elements of strategy combine to steer a business in the right direction and reach its ultimate destination faster and more effectively than its competitors.

Good strategy captures opportunity for improvement, achieves new excellence in operations, builds stronger organizations, helps reduce risk and realizes aspirational visions. Good strategy inspires your colleagues and strengthens your organization's capabilities.

Each individual insight, decision or action contributes to an integrated strategic plan. One of the most important goals of a strategist is to ensure that these discrete elements in the process of strategy are all excellent in their own right. Equally important is to ensure that they bind together to make the value of the whole even greater than the sum of the individual parts.

Strategy is about action and results. Theory, good intentions, detailed documents, glossy presentations and even well thought out strategic designs are never enough. Ideas need to be implemented and results achieved.

As John Gardner stated:

> *In this era of complexity, great enterprises are designed and carried forward by the kind of man who has a vision of what might be and a practical strategy for getting there; a man with an idea in his head and a monkey wrench in his hand.*

These words provide a cogent summary of the spirit and value that can be provided by adopting and implementing an effective strategy program in your own great enterprise.

Statement of Purpose

The specific purpose of this book is to give you a concise and portable guide to the essential elements of successful strategy which are developed more fully in ***STRATEGY: A step-by-step approach to the development and presentation of world class business strategy*** (Palgrave Macmillan, 2004).

It is my hope that, armed with this easy reference, you will be able to improve the quality and content of your own strategies and thus improve substantially on the results achieved in the very real markets in which you operate.

Part I. History and Overview

I.I Lessons from the Past

Element 1: Missing Elements of Traditional Strategy

The complexity of dynamic global markets, accelerated change and the new pressures placed on businesses today have fundamentally reshaped the process and content of successful strategy.

In order to respond properly to these new challenges and build a robust model for future business success, it is now necessary for managers to identify and address seven missing elements of traditional strategic models.

- Comprehensive nature
- Flexibility
- Creativity
- Integration
- Motivation
- Responsibility
- Effectiveness

1. Comprehensive Nature of Change Required for Effective Strategy

Good strategy requires constant and comprehensive change. Priorities need to be more clearly articulated in a world of seemingly unending choice. Real, tangible and sustainable differentiation is essential in an ever more crowded competitive arena. Strategic planning cycles and response times need to be shorter. Manpower allocation needs to be addressed as a matter of the highest priority. The organizations of tomorrow may well have fewer, more skilled people in a more technologically enabled paradigm. Yet, at the same time, a broader set of individuals within the organization, and perhaps even a broader set of organizations, may need to be involved in the process of setting and implementing strategy.

New and more effective measures of success need to be established. New organizational models that cut across or break down established hierarchies may need to be defined and adopted. There is no limit to the areas of potential improvement.

2. Flexibility Demanded by a Rapidly Changing Environment

While it is important to pursue a path of high quality, structured analysis and inclusive procedures, it is also essential to avoid prescribing in advance every detail of a strategy.

Creativity, flexibility and success often go hand in hand. There needs to be room for adjustment in your strategy and enough flexibility in your approach to respond to unexpected external and internal events and actions. Strategies are like living things and need to be able to adapt to survive and prosper.

3. Creativity Essential for Maximum Advantage

Creative breakthrough thinking needs to be encouraged throughout the strategy process.

Leadership needs to be more inspirational and leaders need to encourage individuals to give their very best, even if that means challenging deeply held beliefs and changing long-established practices.

Visions, initiatives and priorities need to be set and maintained, but space also needs to be created for innovation, adaptation, evolution and rejuvenation of supportive activities. Inspirational and creative processes can turbo-charge performance when new risks emerge or new opportunities arise for positive change.

No renaissance is built on a foundation of worn out ideas. True results can only be achieved with a new approach to strategy and an open mind to the real potential for creative and productive change in a constantly evolving business paradigm.

4. Necessary Integration of Process and Content

Perhaps one of the most important reasons that the traditional tools of strategy have lost their cutting edge is that management too often severs process and content. By reintegrating the two in a better approach to strategy, managers will be able to overcome many of the limitations of the past.

The output of good strategy leads to positive individual actions, aligned behind a single, shared vision, fully supporting an agreed strategic plan. This outcome, only possible through an approach which integrates process and content, can add enormously to the force and spirit for profitable change across an entire business.

5. Missing Motivation—The Necessary Human Dimension to Strategy

Another weakness in past models of strategy has been the insufficient attention paid to the human aspects of a business.

By neglecting the aspirational and motivational elements that lie at the heart of every business, many strategies failed to create the energy for change which could make all the difference in a world of ever more intense competition.

Only strategies that take into account this necessary human dimension will be able to realize the full potential of an enterprise. Investing to imbue a sense of individual purpose and accomplishment is an essential element of great and enduring strategy.

Understanding the true beliefs, attitudes, aspirations and capabilities of colleagues, and responding properly, may be the most positive contribution a leader can make to a business.

6. Responsibility Not Integrated into Core Strategy

Failure to build corporate responsibility into a core strategy can be a costly mistake. Unnecessary risks can ripen into environmental, legal or reputational catastrophes.

Less responsible corporate brands and business systems will forfeit revenues which a more esteemed enterprise could attract. A reputation as an uncaring company can even repel some of the most promising young employees.

Forward-thinking strategies integrate responsibility with cutting edge strategy—maximizing profits and creating competitive advantage while operating in a manner which is sensitive to the environment, the workplace and the communities in which businesses operate. The best leaders embed these values within the core strategies and operating principles of a business.

More enlightened managers will extend the notion of responsibility across their full business system, encouraging suppliers, partners and even customers to operate with a more responsible and engaged approach to business. The critical elements of corporate responsibility are examined in more detail in Part II.II of this book.

7. Unacceptable Results from Ineffective Strategies

Finally, and most importantly, a rethink of strategy is needed because the application of an older generation of models has frequently failed to create differentiated performance in the real world.

Implementation may lag behind plans which were never truly executable in the first place. Perhaps the shortage of great business success stories and the decline of so many once great business enterprises are enough to make us question the foundations of many historic approaches to business strategy.

Strategy is a dynamic and evolving discipline. Only by viewing the past clearly and critically can we chart a way forward to the best possible future.

Element 2: Traditional Models of Strategy

Seven traditional models of strategic analysis can provide some useful contributions to a more modern and complete approach to strategy. Each of these models represents a high point of strategic insight at a particular point in the past.

Understanding their sources, application and purpose may stimulate strategic thinking, generate creative tactical ideas and underpin efforts to restore growth or to improve profitability in a business. Most importantly, an understanding of their strengths and weaknesses will provide valuable knowledge for today's strategy.

However, to unlock the full potential of your business you will need to go well beyond the demonstrated limitations of these past approaches.

- The 3C's
- The 5 Forces
- The 7S's
- The 3S's: Single-Shot Strategy
- The 8 Strategic Laws of Gravity
- The 9S's
- The 7C's

1. The 3C's Model

This simple model of business definition drove much strategic thinking in the 1970s and early 1980s.

Following the expansion of the 1960s and in the wake of the 1973 oil shock, many companies needed to redefine their businesses and restructure their diversified portfolios in order to become more competitive. The model generated to serve that purpose was the 3C's model, designed principally to shape understanding of the borders of independent strategic business units and support portfolio restructuring.

- Costs
- Customers
- Competitors

Costs reflect the nature and proportion of economic activity within an organization.

Customers are the group whose needs are served by the entire business system of a company.

Competitors are the set of companies pursuing the same opportunities within a defined geographic or product market.

A lack of sharing in all or many of these three categories meant that the businesses were essentially separate entities and probably could—and should—be managed as separate strategic units. In many cases, the clarity provided by the application of a 3C's business definition exercise allowed large conglomerates to reshape their portfolios, focus their activities and strengthen a set of fewer, but more successful, business units.

A 3C's business definition exercise should not be static. Its value increases dramatically as the dynamic aspects of business evolution are fully considered. A forward-looking business definition can identify emerging changes in the environment which may, in turn, change the nature of your strategy.

The application of business definition can provide greater clarity to business portfolios and lead to more efficient allocations of staff, capital and other corporate resources for future advantage.

2. The 5 Forces Model

In his best-selling book, *Competitive Strategy*, Michael Porter outlined the 5 Forces that drive competitive strategies within a properly defined industry.

An enlightened management approach reflecting the understanding of these industrial forces can lead to superior competitive performance and can generate higher and more sustainable financial returns to stake-holders in the enterprise.

- Entry of new competitors
- Threat of substitutes
- Bargaining power of buyers
- Bargaining power of suppliers
- Rivalry among existing competitors

Destabilizing and costly, the *entry of new competitors* in an industry usually requires a response that will absorb scarce resources and reduce overall returns.

Pricing, and therefore profitability, is influenced by *the threat of substitutes*. Buyers weigh choices which include products which could become available in the future. Competitive gaming will thus be influenced by an understanding of the full set of products potentially available to buyers, not just a limited perspective on what is currently on offer in the market today.

The third competitive force is the *bargaining power of buyers*. The ability of customers to change supplier behavior, primarily through pricing and terms that change the supplier's cost base, has a big effect on the economics of all firms in an industry. The relative power of supplier and buyer can make some industries more attractive and others far less interesting. Major differences can appear in the same industry across geographies. In some industries, this force is clearly the dominant driver of overall profitability and segment attractiveness.

Just as buyers will use their influence to drive supplier behavior, the *bargaining power of suppliers* will do the same when and where possible, exploiting the benefits of opposing strengths and strategic positions. Microsoft, Intel and other tough-minded suppliers can often dictate individual terms and even influence the nature and evolution of an entire industry. Differing concentrations of the supplier base, control of scarce supply, substitutability and other factors can drive a competitive industrial dynamic to very different outcomes.

Rivalry among existing competitors will set the competitive rules which shape behavior and establish investment policies and return patterns across an industry. All elements of the business value chain are directly and profoundly influenced by the nature and intensity of existing industry competitors.

Originally seen as descriptive, or as primarily indicative of an industry's potential to earn returns above the cost of capital, these 5 Forces can also be understood and integrated into a winning competitive strategy.

Although Professor Porter did not specifically link the 5 Forces to a predetermined set of firm strategies, he did map out three generic approaches for successful competitive strategy: differentiation, cost-based leadership and focus.

3. The 7S's Model

The 7S's model, associated primarily with the consulting firm McKinsey and Company, resulted from a fusion of insights that emerged from working sessions between a group of strategic consultants and academics.

The final 7S's—*Strategy, Structure, Systems, Staff, Skills, Style and Shared value*—have been a staple of most strategic diets for a long time and still inform many approaches to organizational design and strategic review. The 7S's model, due to its significance, will be addressed separately in Element 3.

4. The 3S's: Single-Shot Strategy

Many popular business authors purport to capture the essence of strategy in a simple word, concept, or theme.

A single-shot strategy attempts to reduce the complex nature of strategy to an artificially narrow concept and, in the process, reduces the value of a more thorough approach.

- Reengineering
- Total quality management
- Time to market
- Target return on capital
- Six Sigma

In fact, not all of these conceptual prescriptions are as fresh as their purported creators would like us to think. Many of these buzzwords and standards are, to some extent, old wine in a new bottle. They can describe valuable initiatives and focus operating plans. They may contribute to significant improvements in manufacturing quality and overall business performance. But their application does not provide the full benefits of complete strategy.

Most single-shot strategies are focused solely on changes in internal operations and do not address such essential strategic issues as competition or industrial evolution, thereby missing out on key elements of business risk and opportunity. Nor does their content usually link to other aspects of a complete strategy program, such as visionary leadership. These narrow concepts may be worth considering in some cases, but only as a part of a larger and more complete strategic formulation.

5. The 8 Strategic Laws of Gravity

The origins of the 8 Strategic Laws of Gravity model stem from the diagnostic models and data bases on corporate profitability which evolved in the 1970s and 1980s.

Driven by such pioneering concepts as experience curves, growth-share matrices, relative market share/return on sales frameworks and other approaches, the 8 Strategic Laws of Gravity model is more substantial and prescriptive than its predecessors.

Respecting all of these insights in a coordinated approach has allowed many business leaders to set out a more successful competitive strategy.

- Correct business definition
- Market control and leadership
- Incremental share to the leader
- Relative competitive position, performance, and investment
- Declining costs and prices
- Discouraging competitor investment
- Industry value chain and profit pool
- Organization investment

Each of the 8 Laws contains both a descriptive and prescriptive element.

Correct business definition. Understanding the true borders of a business, now and in the future, is critical. As business definition evolves, strategy needs to follow, or even lead, the process of change.

Market control and leadership. When properly defined, a market-leading position can drive shareholder value to the highest possible level. Niche or scale leadership can each provide an avenue to superior financial performance.

Incremental share to the leader. Incremental share gain can be of great value—reinforcing leadership, adding to profits and building a platform for future market power and influence.

Relative competitive position, performance, and investment. Historical analyses, from the early PIMS database to more modern studies of industrial economics, show that relative share within a defined market usually determines relative financial return. An absolute revenue share of 30 percent in a market has enormously different strategic and financial characteristics if that same share creates strong leadership or only a weak trailing position against an even larger competitor.

Declining costs and prices. Originally uncovered in the analysis of input, cost and time efficiencies in the production of military aircraft during the Second World War, the predictable decline in real unit costs and prices with accumulated experience has proven to be a universal micro-economic truth. From pencils to computing power, this same phenomenon is consistently visible across industries, countries, businesses and time. Although the roots of this insight are not new, understanding and managing it continue to be critical elements of successful modern strategy.

Discouraging competitor investment. Strategic cost management, marketing, capital investment, service excellence, brand and channel power, customer management and technological application can discourage competitors from entry into a firm's most profitable market segments. The cost of early dissuasion is usually far lower than the cost of a long future of intensified competition.

Industry value chain and profit pool. Mapping out the sum of profits across an industry or along a business value chain is a critical element of effective strategy. Originally articulated in the Harvard Business Review by two authors from Bain & Company, the profit pool has already become a core concept in modern strategy.

Organizational investment. All of the preceding laws of gravity can best be pursued through superior capabilities, more effective organizational structures and more efficient human resource and management systems.

Failure to invest sufficiently to develop and motivate individuals and teams ensures underperformance in a critical source of potentially great strategic value.

6. The 9S's Model

Japanese strategic consultant Shintaro Hori added two extensions to the traditional 7S's model: *Steering Pattern* and *Syndication*.

- Strategy
- Structure
- Systems
- Style
- Staff
- Skills
- Shared values

+

- Steering pattern
- Syndication

Derived from Hori's observations of failed multinational strategies in Japan, the *Steering Pattern* adds a new dimension to the systems and shared values of an organization. It reflects the universal need to develop and implement a consistent model of leadership and operating culture which communicates how leadership expects results to be achieved at all levels of an organization and across all locations.

Syndication captures a whole wave of change and the potential for creative alliances across old business borders. Syndication parcels out risk to more than one company, redefining the value chain and creatively combining and recombining business assets and processes.

Modern companies are constantly searching for new avenues to create competitive advantage, reduce costs, improve return on capital and share risk burdens where individual scale will not allow any one company to shoulder the entire responsibility for a significant operation or investment.

Adding syndication to the classic 7S's model captures this new area of shared initiatives which did not fit neatly into pre-existing categories of structure or systems.

7. The 7C's Model

The 7C's model of strategy is an enhanced version of the 3C's model of business definition described above, expanding the list of elements to create a more precise definitional model and a more useable set of strategic building blocks. The 7C's model, with the additional elements of *Results*, is addressed more fully in Element 13.

Element 3: The 7S's Model

The 7S's have provided a more comprehensive framework for strategy than many other models. While somewhat vague in providing specific direction, the components of this model can serve as a useful checklist in a more thorough and precise strategy program.

Perhaps because of its general nature and broad conceptual coverage, the framework has not been able to generate a consistently better set of competitive results for many who have attempted to use it in the definition and implementation of a winning strategy.

- Strategy
- Structure
- Systems
- Staff
- Skills
- Style
- Shared values

1. Strategy

The coherent decisions and actions taken to create relative advantage against competitors and improved relations with customers. Resource allocation is a key part of this process.

2. Structure

The organizational structure and operating approach that clarify tasks, responsibilities and roles in the corporate hierarchy.

3. Systems

The procedures, processes and flows of activity that allow an organization to operate.

4. Staff

The people who make up the organization, individually and collectively.

5. Skills

The capacities and capabilities of an organization and its ability to get things done.

6. Style

The behavior of the leadership and therefore usually also of the body of an organization. An organization's style or culture frames the way it acts under different circumstances.

7. Shared Values

The mix of explicit and implied values and goals. Not confined to mission or value statements, shared values are internalized in a business and guide its behavior.

Element 4: Sources of Insight

There are at least seven primary sources of knowledge and wisdom which contribute to the creation of the modern art and science of strategy: grand military strategy, the martial arts, micro- and macro-economics, science, psychology, politics, experience and intuition.

Mastery and application of these separate disciplines on an integrated basis can contribute enormously to the design and execution of successful business strategy.

- Grand military strategy
- The martial arts
- Economics
- Principles of science
- Psychology
- Politics
- Experience and intuition

1. Grand Military Strategy

At the highest level, there is much in common between military and business strategy. Grand military strategy is about the overarching vision of a campaign, the formulation of campaign objectives and a winning approach to a war or series of conflictual engagements. Military strategy includes the gathering of information and intelligence, the formation of alliances, the mustering and management of resource and materiel, the selection and training of manpower, the selection of sites and nature of battle and the setting of rules of engagement.

Grand military strategy, like business strategy, is often as much about winning the hearts and minds of your armies as it is about the scientific principles regarding the deployment of weapons or the engagement of enemy troops.

2. The Martial Arts

The Chinese military sage Sun Tzu is perceived by many strategists as the leading proponent of Asian military strategy at a grand level, but the Japanese sword master Miyamoto Musashi is perhaps equally esteemed as a master of individual combat. This 17th century author of the famed Book of Five Rings (*Go Rin No Sho*), has played an important role in the history of strategy.

Miyamoto Musashi's guide to sword fighting strategy demonstrates the need for a comprehensive understanding of all aspects of life—and of your competitors—to develop *The Way of Strategy*. Through *The Way*, an opponent's likely moves can be predicted and a warrior can engage in individual combat with his position strengthened by advance knowledge and a pre-planned approach to each situation.

The Japanese art of sword combat, Kendo, like all martial arts includes a vital element of reaching deep into the self to access great reserves of force and power; the deeper the personal engagement, the greater the force available to support focused action, powerful impact and needed change.

3. Economics

The dismal science is the source of much strategic knowledge. From the macro-economic views on industrial economics and sources of national competitive advantage to the micro-economic principles of equilibrium pricing, the econometric and theoretical aspects of economics can be played out as useful sources of strategic insight and informed action.

4. Principles of Science

The fundamental principles of science and the particular discipline of dynamic systems behavior underlie many principles associated with strategy. Momentum, focus of force, conservation of energy, inertia and thermodynamic efficiency can be applied to extract useful operating insights leading to profitable action.

A diffusion or inadequacy of energy, contrary or misaligned effort and a failure to respect the fundamental principles of "strategic gravity" can lead to a painful and expensive lesson for uninformed strategists.

To effect change across a large organization characterized primarily by resistance and inertia, managers must take into account the amount of energy required to get the whole system moving at the right speed and in the right direction. Similarly, if a business is way off track, its leaders will need to invest sufficient energy—human, financial, and operational—to get the business back on the correct pathway.

5. Psychology

Ego, identity, ambition, interaction, belief, attitude and behavior are all inextricably intertwined with the strategies and operations of any business, no matter how large or small. Whether related to motivating individuals and teams, organizing collective endeavors, communicating effectively, or managing a whole enterprise, within every effective strategy lie many elements of psychology.

To take one example, the documented human responsive cycle of shock, denial, anger, depression and acceptance is but one of the many patterns of behavior which has been effectively transplanted from the realm of clinical psychology to modern business strategy. Observed initially in patients who had received a negative prognosis on their health, the same predictable pattern of behavior is observed—and hence managed—in organizations facing great change, such as a business facing merger, sale, reduction in size or a major change in established operating practice.

6. Politics

Just as politics, especially international politics, is about consolidation, alliances, interconnection and the unending competition for resources, economic advantage and growth, the same is true of businesses.

Political science is relevant to both the internal and external operations of an enterprise. Externally, relationships with governments, regulators, shareholders, customers and suppliers call into play the full range of a manager's political skills. Internally, politics are an inevitable part of corporate life.

One great entrepreneur once described an organization without politics as a frictionless machine—great in theory but non-existent in the real world.

7. Experience and Intuition

While there are strategic insights to be gained from military, scientific, political and other sources of knowledge, there is always room for creativity and insight based on individual experience and intuition.

By looking at other examples of inspired creativity, new thinking and unanticipated action, much can be learned. New strategic approaches can be evolved with the right degree of creativity, customization and adaptation.

None of the individual sources of knowledge defined above can provide a pre-packaged, off-the-shelf strategy. Good strategy draws from all of these sources and is then tempered and shaped by experience, creativity and intuition.

If we compare the rich depths of these seven sources of strategic insight and inspiration to the reductive models applied by many businesses today, we can see how great is the potential for more aspirational business visions and more successful corporate strategies.

By drawing from a deeper well we can discover fresh and exciting ideas that can refresh our strategies and improve dramatically on the results we achieve for all of our stakeholders.

I.II Phases of Strategy

Element 5: Respecting Process Principles

One of the greatest failings in traditional models of business strategy is a lack of specificity in addressing the elements of the strategic process.

A great American legal philosopher and jurist once stated that "good process makes good law". The same is true regarding strategy. By following the best possible process you will be far more likely to achieve the best possible results.

- Ensure an effective process
- Ensure an inclusive process
- Set long-term objectives
- Test the logic and the process
- Balance planning with flexibility
- Search for creativity
- Embrace risk

1. Ensure an Effective Process

Many strategic planning processes are efficient rather than effective. Timetables are brisk. Review sessions are short. Feedback is focused. The process is rushed, mechanical and uninspiring. The linear and nonlinear character of modern strategy may require further discussion from fresh perspectives and may even demand more challenge on the overarching vision than these brisk processes allow.

An effective process may take longer and absorb more scarce resources, but in the end it is the results achieved that matter, not the speed at which the process operates.

2. Ensure an Inclusive Process—Break Down the Hierarchy

One proven way to increase the creative output of a high-quality organization is to break down line and staff barriers in the strategy process. A combined team of finance, marketing and line managers may be far more effective than a purely marketing-led view of the competition. Creative teaming can also break down external and internal walls. Involving suppliers and customers may elicit win–win opportunities and surface new opportunities to create competitive advantage.

Strategies can benefit enormously from the informed perspectives of other players in the value chain. Entire books have been written on the value of including customers in strategy formulation. Suppliers as well can produce good ideas, align economic activities and restructure trade terms for mutual benefit. With the greatest degree of caution, selected competitors may also cooperate in setting some parts of strategy, a trend which has spawned the new word "comperation", a positive synthesis of the traditionally antagonistic concepts of competition and cooperation.

3. Set Long-term Objectives for Individuals and the Group

A full view of strategy may also require objectives to be set and investments made which will only show benefits over a much longer time frame.

Multi-year action plans and targets may be required for major investment, marketing or operating initiatives, for individual and group development plans and for organizational change programs.

Longer term objectives could include revenue and profit targets, market share targets, improvements in customer satisfaction scores, systems implementation, team skills development, hiring targets, individual skill development programs, industry consolidation objectives and other essential strategic targets.

The establishment and communication of these longer term objectives provide valuable opportunities for senior managers to engage, direct and motivate their colleagues.

4. Test the Logic and the Process

Good strategy can be characterized as an inexorable flow of logic from insight to action; a seamless web of facts, principles, decisions and actions that allows an organization to achieve its most ambitious goals and generate extraordinary returns.

In order to ensure that your strategy is indeed world class, all aspects of your strategic logic should be constantly tested, cross-examined and challenged. Where necessary, change should be made as early as possible.

5. Balance Strategic Planning with Strategic Flexibility

Business strategy today can be more like a sweaty wrestling match than an elegant ballet choreographed in advance. Modern approaches may require responsive, as well as planned out, initiatives.

Professor Moshe Rubinstein described the need of modern strategy to be “half planned and half unplanned”, executing on well thought through initiatives but always ready to respond to the unexpected.

The final content of a sound strategic document should be architectural rather than exhaustive. It should describe the vision, principles and precise goals. It should outline plans for action. Yet the final details, engineering and the detailed plans may need to be developed and implemented flexibly over time.

6. Search for Nonlinearity and Creative Breakthroughs

World class strategy maximizes the benefits of past experience and learning, but also prepares an organization for the new and the unexpected. The environment will always produce surprises and those surprises may well require significant strategic change or redirection.

Good strategies will benefit from fast response to change and may even deliberately create and exploit discontinuity for individual advantage. By understanding the multi-dimensional and interdependent nature of events and business systems, talented management teams will be able to foresee and profit from the opportunities inherent in any period of discontinuous change, turbulence or redefinition.

Winners in the modern business paradigm are systematically able to profit from discontinuous change as and when it occurs.

7. Embrace Risk, Action, and the Acceptance of Failure

Not all efforts will succeed but without risk, trial and some failure, there can only be limited progress. The only way we really learn is through action and experience, both good and bad. In fact, it is perhaps through our worst experiences that we gain the most valuable knowledge. We must be willing to act, test and expand the boundaries of what we know—a healthy process that accepts risk and tolerates some failure to add profitablility to that collective store of knowledge.

By acting with courage and creativity, managers can test ever more aggressively the borders of the possible and magnify the value of their eventual success.

Element 6: Diagnostic Phase

There are three integrated phases of a full strategy program—diagnosis, design and implementation planning. Only by following all three on a fully coordinated basis can a strategy be based on facts, be designed for full and successful implementation and create lasting and tangible benefits for all stakeholders.

The purpose of the diagnostic phase is to clarify all facts related to the historical and current business environment, observe and understand the trends and influences on the future and spell out precisely the options available to the management or ownership team. Only when this phase is concluded can the design and implementation planning phases begin.

- Point of departure
- Portfolio perspective
- Profit pool perspective
- Competitive perspective
- Business dynamics
- Organizational assessment
- Range of strategic options

1. Point of Departure

The first step in a strategy diagnostic is to prepare an analytical summary of the current state of the business in absolute terms and relative to competitors. This point of departure summary will include company history, business definition, an overview of customers, markets and sources of profitability. It will address historical and current financial results, summarize the strategic balance sheet and identify any organizational issues.

2. Portfolio Perspective

The era of businesses attempting to be all things to all people in all places at all times is well and truly over.

Clear strategies require a fresh look at the collection of businesses and activities being pursued. The value of the entire portfolio as a system needs to be assessed as well as looking at each separate business unit.

Assessing competitiveness by analyzing both business unit and business process portfolios is essential to provide an internal and external view of the business system:

Business unit portfolio: This typical analytical tool looks at the relative strength and performance of each business unit.

One logical outcome from this perspective is a restructuring of the portfolio of businesses to focus resources only on those selected strategic business units (SBUs) that can create the highest economic value for stakeholders.

By eliminating low yield activities, adding to profitable businesses and focusing investment, a senior management team can lift the performance of a collection of businesses to a much higher level.

Business process portfolio: Restructuring an internal portfolio of activities can also lead to a more efficient business model. Analysis can lead to spinning off processes, outsourcing, combining entities, insourcing, reengineering and pursuing corporate transformation programs.

3. Profit Pool Perspective

It is no longer enough to analyze only the traditional view of profits earned by a business in a modern industry. All sources of current and potential profit—taking into account both external and internal profit pool perspectives—need to be analyzed, understood and acted upon.

The external profit pool is a perspective which analyzes the total pool of profits along the whole value chain of an industry from raw material suppliers through to end customers, incorporating all relevant products and services along the way.

The internal profit pool is a complementary view which analyzes the sources of profitability within the current and future business model.

The insights from this twin approach can lead to significant action. Many automotive and component companies, appliance manufacturers and electronic goods retailers now make far more money from a focus on services, warranties and finance fees than on new product sales.

4. Competitive Perspective

One of the most common failings of modern corporate strategists is to underinvest in an understanding of competitors.

By fully analyzing competitors, opportunities to learn from—and to exploit—their weaknesses can emerge. Two particular areas to address include:

Competitor SWOT. Strategists must think through the complete competitor perspective, addressing strengths, weaknesses, opportunities and threats and then attack the weak points in the strategy of selected competitors in a focused and effective manner.

Standards of operating excellence. By benchmarking leading competitors' achievements to reset higher standards for your own business and by defining target contra-actions, managers will be far more able to implement their own successful strategies.

5. Business Dynamics

Every business sits amid a constant flow of external events and systems which affect its performance and influence its activities.

An ability to see the future more clearly than your competitors is one of your most powerful weapons, allowing you to spot and exploit profitable opportunities and anticipate future risks by effective action. By mastering the flow of the dynamic elements of your business "eco-system", you will be able to stay on top of business challenges now and in the future.

6. Organizational Assessment

Making a tough and honest assessment of your organization and the individuals within it is one of the most valuable and most difficult aspects of strategy.

Acting early to address people issues can have enormous long-term benefit. A thorough, data-driven assessment should include organizational structure, operating principles, collective capabilities, values, culture, satisfaction and a framework to manage individual performance and capability.

7. Range of Strategic Options

At the end of the diagnostic phase, the full range of real strategic options should be set out, based on the preceding analytical steps.

Strategic options should usually be confined to six or fewer summary approaches through a process of discussion and evaluation. In the process, some actions can be reallocated from one option to another, and labels rewritten to reflect progress in understanding.

While there is an infinite number of potential detailed strategies for any one business, clear thought can usually group actions under a few coherent strategic options which may include such initiatives as major cost reduction, sale of a business, reduction to a smaller core of businesses, investing for rapid organic growth, merger or acquisition, adding international markets or careful diversification.

Element 7: Design Phase

Based upon the facts and observations gleaned in the diagnostic phase, the design phase will draw together all elements of your strategy into a single coherent approach, leading seamlessly from insight to implementation.

In order to be as powerful and effective as it possibly can, the design phase must be carried out with one eye on the lessons of the past and another on the demands of the future.

- The promise
- Key levers on performance and value
- Priorities and resource allocation
- Strategic option selection
- New organizational approach
- Risk management
- Target results

1. The Promise

Going beyond the traditional, and possibly over-used, label of 'vision statement', *The Promise* carries with it a greater sense of commitment and a more personal depth of feeling. By making *The Promise* there is an opportunity for business leaders to address a broader set of challenges, to reach the heart and soul of an enterprise and the people within it.

The Promise is perhaps the most important element in any strategy as it sets the overarching goal that will unite and motivate employees behind a common purpose, guide investment decisions and both inform and inspire all stakeholders.

There are four key elements of *The Promise*: a clear vision, a detailed mission statement, a commitment to values and a program of engagement and responsibility.

2. Key Levers on Performance and Value

Within each industry, there is a limited set of high impact 'levers' that can lift business performance most efficiently and effectively. These levers can include high market share, low cost position, superior product quality and service, effective customer segmentation and other elements.

Once the key levers have been identified, the task is to define how they can best be applied to create the greatest positive impact for your organization. The resulting imperatives will serve as a bridge between a more general vision and specific priorities, operating targets and investments.

3. Priorities and Resource Allocation

The best approach to achieving an actionable set of priorities needs to be worked through step by step.

First, make a comprehensive list of potential priorities which focus on the levers of performance and value. Second, place each on a priority framework which rates the expected value of each initiative against the estimated difficulty to implement. Third, select priorities, drawing a line between those initiatives which will be pursued and those which will not. Last, allocate resources.

A clearly defined set of priorities (and an equally clearly defined set of non-priorities) can guide resource allocation to those areas that will lead to the highest return on corporate and human capital.

4. Strategic Option Selection

This stage involves valuing the range of options specified at the end of the diagnostic phase and spelling out the pros and cons of each. Although there are many potential options, most real options can be captured in a limited set of choices.

Options should include sale (which is always an option), status quo (which is infrequently chosen), and a focused set of intermediate options with ascending degrees of change, perceived risk and return.

By allocating actions and initiatives to clearly labelled options, the senior team will be more capable of understanding and debating the relative merits of each of the options proposed.

After selecting a single option, the senior team should ensure that it will indeed lead to the achievement of *The Promise* set out earlier.

5. New Organizational Approach

As businesses refocus on a limited set of priority actions, organizations must bring to bear their full capabilities in key areas, intensifying targeted efforts and operating more effectively on a coordinated, global basis.

Organizational issues can be extremely complex and multifaceted. In designing the best model to implement your strategy and to achieve operating targets, the leadership team may well need to proceed on many fronts at the same time. This may require selecting the best model of organization, acting to improve capability, changing people as needed, addressing needs for culture change and perhaps even implementing a values migration program across an entire organization.

There are three parts to organizational design: structure, staffing and operating principles. All three phases are essential to ensure that options can be implemented in a way that suits the unique culture and character of a company.

6. Risk Management

Every strategy carries with it a set of risks which require analysis and management. There is no such thing as a low risk/high return strategy in most industries. The bolder the proposed change, the greater the risks involved.

Unbundling the elements of risk and opportunity will result in a more scientific definition which allows management teams to know where resources can best be deployed to reduce risk and exploit opportunity.

Business risks can broadly be broken down into three categories: financial, operating and contextual. A far-sighted team will have a specific plan of action in all of these areas.

7. Target Results

Successful strategies can only be driven by managers with a clear set of targets indicating the performance required to implement the chosen strategy. These targets must be ambitious, credible and fully aligned with the agreed strategy.

Target results to measure success or failure include quantified measures for the key levers as described above, financial results, cash flow, strategic balance sheet and the proven impact of strategic initiatives on competitive and market position.

In the spirit of focusing on priorities and investing differentially in a select set of levers on performance and value, it is useful to confirm that there is at least one target result for each lever and priority identified.

Element 8: Implementation Phase

Immediately upon concluding the design phase, implementation planning needs to begin. In the previous two phases the priority imperatives and actions needed to make your strategy a reality should have become clear and well documented.

The bridge between thought and action is one of the most important characteristics of the overall strategy process. The implementation planning phase addresses the actions, team and resources necessary to implement the strategy. This phase also sets up the strategic dashboard necessary to monitor progress, apply corrective management and outline an effective approach to leadership and communication.

The implementation plan should be a natural consequence of strategic design, the culmination of that inexorable flow of logic from insight to focused action in the market.

- Imperatives, actions, responsibilities
- Tactics and timetable
- Implementation team
- Alignment and integration
- Program control
- Full value capture
- Leadership and motivation

1. Imperatives, Actions, Responsibilities

By stating the required imperatives and actions to realize your vision and then allocating specific responsibility to each, you will be able to link the diagnosis, design and implementation phases of your strategy.

There are three components to this first step of the implementation phase: a summary of all imperatives, an allocation of individual responsibility, and a high level schedule of implementation, taking into account all relevant factors.

Ensuring that each executive has signed up to his or her responsibilities, and has agreed implementation deadlines, should conclude the first step in a successful phase of implementation.

2. Tactics and Timetable

Each proposed initiative or action can be pursued through a wide range of tactical approaches. Choosing the best approach will have a major bearing on the success of the entire strategy. Poorly chosen tactics, ranging from team leadership choices to incorrect timing, or from insufficient allocation of resource to failure to plan for contingencies, can reduce the effectiveness of the investment or even lead to total strategic failure. Element 18 expands on the constituent elements of tactics.

Of all tactical elements, timing may be the most important. Only by considering all aspects of an initiative can the most advantageous timetable be set.

3. Implementation Team

Some strategy exercises will require the constitution of a separate project team dedicated to the diagnosis, design and implementation of the strategic plans. Others will require staff to reallocate time to accommodate strategy-related activities.

Because good strategy is holistic, the strategy team's membership should be cross-functional, including members with varying backgrounds, jobs and expertise.

Where there are resource gaps, insufficient skills or a limited time frame, a specific program of resource acquisition will be required.

4. Alignment and Integration

It is essential to align all aspects of the strategic business system. To implement a chosen strategy requires that all barriers and inconsistencies be removed and all organizational forces applied in the same direction. Too often, ambitious visions fail to materialize because there is insufficient resource dedicated, contrary initiatives underway, misalignment of activities, or a missing element of organizational integration necessary to implement the supporting strategies.

The integration process will need to review top-down and bottom-up perspectives on a strategy repeatedly and in ever finer detail. Such a detailed and comprehensive view will be needed to confirm that all wrinkles are ironed out and all opportunities for synergies fully exploited.

5. Program Control

One of the reasons many businesses do not achieve the visionary ambitions of their leaders is that feedback systems, usually in the form of management information systems, are incomplete or "tuned in to the wrong station".

Too often there is both a data overload and an insufficient amount of useable information. To ensure success, you will benefit from creating a custom-designed strategic dashboard which identifies and monitors progress against critical target results, timetables for specific actions and expected outcomes from those actions.

Those initiatives which are significantly off-track or repeatedly failing to meet deadlines will require the attention of senior management and may also require that appropriate corrective action is taken. Resources can be reallocated, sanctions for underperformance meted out, or a better approach agreed and new objectives and deadlines set.

6. Full Value Capture

Full value capture is one of the most important and least understood steps in maximizing the value of strategy. Many strategies, even when well designed and executed, fail to yield their maximum benefit due simply to a lack of explicit effort to capture their full value.

External benefits may be lost simply because the full value of the strategic advances in capital markets, with customers, or with suppliers is not identified. Internal value is lost when valuable learning is not captured, best practices are not documented and organizational heroics are not sufficiently rewarded.

There are at least seven sources of potential value that can be enhanced or realized through a comprehensive value screen: content, customer, capability, capital, future option, contingent and full systemic value.

7. Leadership and Motivation

Effective leadership will require the application of a full complement of leadership skills, setting an example of dedication, demonstrating proper values, communicating effectively, setting targets, working with internal and external constituencies and providing central guidance to the overall process.

Strategy programs require both visible leadership—action-oriented leadership from the front—and supportive leadership from behind the scenes to ensure the best outcome.

Inspiration and personal engagement are essential to generate the best possible results at each stage in a strategy process. The highest performance for an organization is only possible if the hearts and minds of the individuals within it are fully captured by the vision, the strategy, the plan of action and the leadership of the strategy exercise. These elements will be described in greater detail in Part II.III of this book.

Element 9: Documenting Strategy

The content of your strategy program must be captured accurately and in a manner which will allow easy communication throughout your organization. Failure to do so can significantly reduce its value.

Listed below are some of the key reasons why the ability to document a strategy clearly and succinctly is vital to your strategic success.

- Inspiration and creativity
- Quality of thought
- Communication
- Refinement
- Integration
- Alignment
- Future reference

1. Inspiration and Creativity

The creative process is greatly enhanced by the careful selection of words used to define with precision what the strategy is about. Ideas beget ideas. Words inspire thought. By defining the way forward in writing, new elements will emerge which can enhance the ultimate value of the chosen strategy.

2. Quality of Thought

Writing down the strategy inspires thought, insight and focus. Conflicts and gaps in thinking and proposed action are exposed. The quality of thought is improved.

3. Communication

A written document is essential to communicate your strategy throughout the organization. Its content can be refined through feedback. Necessary buy-in and approval can be achieved. A shared sense of common purpose can be fostered.

The quality of organizational alignment depends, in great measure, on the clarity of communication of the vision and supporting strategy.

4. Refinement

No strategy begins in final form. Documentation will provide a canvas for the filtering, processing and elimination of unwanted elements to refine strategy output and produce the highest quality result.

5. Integration

Marketing, design, production, procurement, service, sales and all other business aspects need to be brought together into one coherent plan to work well. Comprehensive documentation of a strategy allows the integration of all departmental plans to take place more efficiently and effectively.

6. Alignment

A cogent, crisp and concise written summary of your strategy provides the foundation for aligning group and individual objectives across even the largest organization.

Strategies are relevant for all members of an organization, but not everyone can join directly in the steps of diagnosis, design and implementation. For those colleagues who are not part of the core team, or who may have joined a business after the completion of the strategy exercise, the opportunity to access a cogent summary of the strategy can be invaluable in ensuring their own actions are fully in line with group direction.

7. Future Reference

Careful documentation will provide future generations of strategy managers with a reference point to help learn from the past by assessing the success or failure of initiatives undertaken.

Confidentiality: A note of caution

Once a strategy has been documented, it is essential to protect its confidentiality. Leaks can be very expensive indeed.

A tough document management policy will be needed to ensure that strategic value is not diminished or lost altogether by careless or deliberately inappropriate disclosure.

I.III Lessons for the Future

Element 10: Differentiating Characteristics

When compared to past models of strategy, the approach described in this book proceeds in a different manner along seven critical dimensions listed below, addressing the gaps identified in Element 1.

- More comprehensive
- More flexible
- More integrating
- More creative
- More motivating
- More responsible
- More effective

1. More Comprehensive: Integrating Process and Content

The first step in building a better approach to strategy is the fusion of process and content.

In getting better results from your business, how you go about setting and implementing your strategy can be as important as the specific structure of your final plans. By excluding key members of your enterprise from the process, you may be both demotivating those who most need to be motivated. Through their exclusion you may also miss key sources of valuable information and reduce the potential for insights which can drive competitive advantage.

Diagnosis, design, implementation, skill development, resource allocation, leadership and motivation need to be integrated into one indivisible whole. Vision, strategy and tactics need to be reviewed, coordinated, integrated and aligned in a unified approach to achieve full business potential in the real business world.

2. More Flexible: Better Adapted to Accelerating Change

The business landscape is littered with the carcasses of dinosaurs unable to adapt to a new world of rapid change. Linear change is faster. Nonlinear shifts appear abruptly and unexpectedly. Longstanding borders on business and business definitions collapse or erode quickly. Customers and suppliers can become competitors or close collaborators in future strategy. Competitors can become allies or even colleagues in new business paradigms.

Strategy in the business world, as in the natural world, is all about pursuing the best approach to winning the brutal competition for survival and prosperity, or facing inevitable extinction in a remorseless world of natural selection. It is instructive to note that Charles Darwin did not say that only the strongest survive. Darwin actually said, more accurately, that those species which were best adapted to changes in the environment were the most likely to survive.

3. More Integrative: Incorporating Multiple Perspectives

In a complex and dynamic world, multiple perspectives are necessary to understand the full meaning and impact of events taking place within and around an organization. No one person, team, or department will have a monopoly on valuable information or insight into any of the three phases of a full strategy approach. Contributions from more people, embracing diverse sources of perspective and experience, need to be gathered and reviewed to create full understanding.

Only through a thoughtful integration of a sufficiently large set of differing perspectives can a full set of strategic insights be assured.

4. More Creative: Breaking Old Ways of Thinking

Good strategy requires managers to nurture, value and manage intuition and creativity as never before. Experimentation must be encouraged and acceptable levels of failure tolerated. No one ever made great scientific breakthroughs by a system of pure trial and success.

Destroying old models and rejecting well-established practices is never easy. Organizational and staff changes are some of the most difficult decisions to take and to implement in any business environment. Yet without the courage to discard the old, we can never move forward fully into the new.

5. More Motivating: Inspiring as well as Guiding Individuals

The old model of an hour's pay for an hour's labor is no longer enough to retain employees or inspire colleagues in an enterprise to achieve their full potential.

The same is true at a collective level, as engagement in a program of change needs to be presented and pursued in a new and different way. Individuals and entire organizations need to be more fully engaged and better motivated to rise to meet the challenge of world class strategy. A fuller engagement and motivation of key individuals can trigger a quantum leap in the energy available for change, creating competitive advantage and inspiring greater collective performance.

Great leaders in the new business paradigm will go beyond simple resource allocation, the bedrock notion of traditional strategy and, through inspiration, create a whole new level of resource for change in the energy of their people and the motivation of their organizations.

6. More Responsible: Integrating Strategy and Responsibility

By moving faster than the competition in developing responsible strategies, leaders can position their businesses and their brands as more customer and community friendly than their rivals.

Forward thinking leaders can reap the benefits of being an admired and welcome corporate citizen, resident, or guest in all the countries where they chose to operate. They will also benefit by participating at an early stage in the emergence of a more thoughtful model of engagement and responsibility where positive images and actions can now be developed, and seen to be developed, at relatively lower cost than in a more crowded future.

A more responsible business stance can improve relations with customers, suppliers, legislators and regulators. Perhaps most importantly, a proactive approach to responsibility can present opportunities to inspire greater personal engagement and commitment of employees and other stakeholders in your business system.

Leading a company with a conscience and an eye to a healthy bottom line can create very real value for current and future stakeholders.

7. More Effective: Ensuring Implementation to Achieve Tangible Results

Strategies are useful only if they create tangible value in the real world.

The full measure of a new approach to strategy is whether it is more effective than its predecessors, whether the results are better than before and whether the investments to achieve these results are justified by the return. Satisfactory underperformance, a term relating to longstanding practices or standards which have become accepted over time but are, in fact, unacceptable if looked at afresh, must be unveiled in all its forms and addressed directly by effective action, leading to far better results.

Strategies need to be designed for execution. Theories are valuable only when they lead to specific and measurable action.

Indeed, strategies that are not implemented may well carry significant negative value. They carry a high opportunity cost on the management time invested, alienate the most capable employees, add to organizational cynicism and loss of faith in leadership and lead to many lost opportunities in the market place.

Good strategy and effective action go hand in hand.

Element 11: Improving Creativity

Creativity at each step in the process is an essential part of any winning strategy.

In a world where all competitors have equal access to global low cost manufacturing operations, to state-of-the-art technologies and to greater competitive information than ever before, individuals and collective creativity may be the greatest source of competitive advantage.

It is therefore appropriate to consider how to best foster and grow creativity within your organization.

- Brainstorm
- Change the people involved
- Explore new angles
- Avoid insularity
- Meditate
- Look for patterns
- Integrate

1. Brainstorm—Draw on the Power of the Group

Often, the best ideas are sparked by interaction between individuals in a group setting.

Great ideas can come from great people at all levels of the organization. Attempting to confine the process of strategy-setting or isolate creative individuals may well limit the creative potential of the whole. Group brainstorming may generate many good ideas, among them perhaps a few which will truly make a fundamental improvement in your business results.

It is thus important to broaden participation sufficiently and to allocate sufficient unstructured time to brainstorm during or between strategy exercises.

2. Change the People Involved

As so much of creativity is about drawing from a set of differing personal experiences, changing the constitution of the group from time to time can be extremely useful in stimulating new ideas.

New members of a strategic review group can come from within your business, or can be hired in from the outside on a full-time basis. Alternatively, contracted resources can be brought in to assist in the strategic process on a focused basis and then released, without incurring the high costs of hiring and integrating a new full time employee.

3. Explore New Angles—Think from a Competitor's Perspective

During one the largest takeover battles in UK history, a far-sighted CFO appointed one of his cleverest assistants to step down from his daily job and act throughout the contested bid as the opposing bidder would act. He was tasked with thinking through the potential strategies, tactics, pricing limits and alliances of both companies from an entirely different perspective.

The colleague's performance was so effective that the CFO, following a hard fought victory, institutionalized the practice for future takeover initiatives. This same approach could be equally valuable in a non-transactional situation, providing a whole new look at the business and its potential from a different perspective.

4. Avoid Insularity—Extract Lessons from Parallel Industries and Other Areas

It would be a folly to assume that there is only one insight, model, or approach that can lead to creative understanding or improved results. Nor is there any best approach which is fixed in time. There is always an element of change, of adaptation to the unknown and the unexpected.

It is essential always to leave an open space in the thought process to allow applicable new information to come forward from different sources and for further inspiration to flourish as the circle of knowledge grows.

Albert Einstein once said that problems cannot be solved at the level where they arise. By taking a different perspective, we are far more likely to find solutions to even the most intractable of problems, no matter how, when and where they arise.

5. Meditate—Clear your Mind to Make Room for Innovative Ideas

Most of the principles above are either directed at drawing on untapped sources of capability within a firm, or tapping into external sources which can be effectively transferred across a business or industry boundary.

Other sources of creativity are more personal and require a different approach. Meditation, proven to stimulate creative thinking and reduce counter-productive stress, may be the best of these alternative personal approaches.

By clearing your mind from the clutter of daily preoccupations, there is more space available for new insights, for an unhurried balancing of contending ideas, for the discovery of new possiblities and the arrival of fresh perspectives.

Uninterrupted, calm meditation, by any method, adds enormously to the potential for clear and creative strategic thought.

6. Look for Patterns—Understand Systemic Behavior

Much of creativity, as Senge describes in his book *The Fifth Discipline*, is about understanding and responding to systemic patterns of social or economic behavior.

In one memorable article in the *Harvard Business Review*, two experts in the observation and understanding of patterns of avian behavior exhibited in the natural world described the predictability and analytical approaches which could be derived from an understanding of systemic patterns as they emerged.

As the authors of *Spotting Patterns on the Fly* stated "... The ability to grasp complicated phenomena, and discern possible trends from seemingly random events, can be a source of competitive advantage, allowing managers to capitalize on opportunities before they are apparent to others."

7. Integrate—Find New Connections in a Network Paradigm

The notion of integrating disparate disciplines harks back to a period where a few exceptional men were able to benefit from an approach and an attitude that transcended any one discipline or single point of view.

By bringing together studies in science, the arts, culture, philosophy, religion, language, politics, history and engineering, original Renaissance Man was able to open new vistas, to see new connections and to generate new insights and works of art that stand out as some of mankind's greatest achievements.

In today's complex world we all need to think and act like Renaissance men and women to extract the full potential of our modern businesses. Modern management teams could well aspire to learn from *how* these men thought as well as *what* they thought.

Like success, creativity is a journey, not a destination. There is no end to the potential for improvement, growth and greater reward if we apply an integrated view of the new world in which we all compete.

Element 12: Managing Trends and Influences

One of the reasons why traditional strategic models have failed to keep up with the pace of change in the business world is that most are, in essence, static snapshots of businesses which are in a constantly flowing process of change, redefinition and evolution. Old models simply do not work within this new and dynamic paradigm.

Business systems are neither static nor simple and they can now only be addressed on a more holistic and "living" basis. Strategy, reflecting this realization, is also becoming more fluid, more vital and far more capable of acting to profit from complexity and constant change.

There are seven recurring influences in global, social and economic systems that can provide input for a more informed approach to strategic action. These trends combine to create an entirely new business paradigm, the mastering of which is an essential element in developing a winning strategy.

By understanding these trends and influences we can ensure that our businesses are best adapted to changes in the environment and more likely to survive and prosper.

- Globalization
- Complexity and convergence
- Acceleration
- Turbulence
- Connectivity
- Ephemeralization
- Consolidation

1. Globalization

Globalization redefines many of the major sources of business risk and opportunity today.

It is no longer just business entities that are "going global" images, data and information, products, capital, ideas, careers, families, friends and almost anything else you can think of can now be transported with increasing speed and efficiency via delivery, distribution and communication systems that span the world.

The new principle of instantaneous globalization, perhaps the most commonly cited element in the evolution of complex modern businesses and economic systems, constantly creates new strategic challenges.

2. Complexity and Convergence

Modern business is rapidly becoming more complex. Companies are multi-national and transnational. Product and service options proliferate. Logistics, technologies and manufacturing systems flex and evolve globally. Competitors, suppliers, distributors, owners and managers all operate amid perpetual change and growing complexity.

Perhaps the most effective response to complexity is to pursue a clear and compelling vision. Only constant focus on a common goal, supported by up to date information, effective communication and uninterrupted effort can bring about constructive change in any complex dynamic system.

As businesses converge they will look more alike and act more similarly. This paradigm principle is, as one wag put it, "as clear as the Palm in your hand". The world of handheld devices reflects many underlying trends of technological and functional convergence.

As patterns and systems converge, the critical factor for management success is to develop a strategic response to profit from the end-state toward which the systems are converging and to benefit from opportunities created along the way.

3. Acceleration

Not only is change now constant, the pace of change is accelerating in almost every dimension.

The unprecedented pace of technological change accelerates overall change in an already rapidly evolving set of global economic systems. Even Moore's Law, which forecast a doubling of processor power every 18 months, is already long out of date. Each doubling of power has now accelerated to a rate exceeding a 100 percent increase in capability every 12 months. This accelerating pace of change shows no sign of relenting.

Some changes are so profound that they do not just shift a business incrementally. They require discarding old models entirely, rethinking the business and adopting an entirely new approach for the future.

4. Turbulence

Turbulence in the business world occurs where there is dramatic change in the external environment or in the critical variables and functions of an internal system. It is characterized by rapid changes in the regulatory or competitive order, fundamental changes in business definition or dramatic changes in the nature of products, services or distribution systems.

Out of turbulence comes great opportunity for success. The winning formula in times of turbulence is driven by four key factors, all organizational: First, being externally focused and able to track and respond swiftly to changing events. Second, being fast and flexible in response. Third, being long-term in outlook. And fourth, being constantly dissatisfied with the status quo and constantly searching for opportunities to improve future performance.

Organizations need to measure themselves accurately against these four winning characteristics and change how they operate when they fail to attain requisite standards of excellence.

5. Connectivity

The world is more interconnected and with greater rapidity and accuracy than ever before. This trend will continue.

This new state of interconnectedness has been neatly summarized by one of the leading experts and more eloquent spokesmen on the evolution of technology:

> *"We're talking about connecting everything in the world to everything else. That means that every artifact that we make will be embedded with some chip, some little sliver of dim intelligence, maybe only as smart as a bee or an ant. But all of those pieces, some of them moving around and some stationary, will be connected, and will be communicating with each other. So, the graph of the number of things that we make, and the graph of the numbers of things that are*

> *connected, will in the near future converge and meet, and everything we make will be connected to everything else. And that is the network. That is the Net, in the large sense that we talk about."*

A corollary to this increasing connectivity and interconnectedness is interdependence.

From a commercial standpoint, realization of this more interconnected nature of the business world raises a whole new set of challenges. It is more essential than ever to understand and react to external trends and influences by developing future-oriented strategies.

6. Ephemeralization

Ephemeralization is the process of becoming less physical and more virtual in manifestation.

Expounded by R. Buckminster Fuller in the 1960s, this paradigm principle can be seen in system after system in the modern business world. For example, in modern telecommunications (with small, mobile, wireless handsets operating virtually instantaneously), finance (who goes into a branch for assisted cash withdrawals any more?), retail (with online shopping) and computers (ever more portable and more powerful). In his view, many systems and connected networks were becoming less present, even as their functionality increased.

In this ephemeral world it is essential to anticipate change, recognize future trends and invest to create the maximum competitive advantage out of inevitable change.

7. Consolidation

In many businesses today there is a visible trend toward consolidation of formerly independent suppliers, competitors and customers into larger unified blocks. This can be seen at national and international level as mergers and acquisitions combine ever larger players into single units.

This trend may profoundly affect your business. You may have to consider participating in industry-defining mergers and acquisitions yourself, or face the prospect of a future contending against bigger and more powerful rivals.

The organizational implications are also significant. In order to effect a successful merger or acquisition your team will need to develop the skills of acquiring and integrating other corporate entities.

The automobile, pharmaceutical, energy, banking, insurance, telecommunications, steel, component, advertising, chemical, accounting, aircraft, defense and countless other industries are all on highly visible pathways to greater consolidation and concentration.

Element 13: The 7C's Model + Results

As already stated in Element 2, the 7C's model can provide a powerful framework to define more precisely the borders of a business, evaluate core strategic options and identify and prioritize adjacent growth opportunities.

- Costs
- Customers
- Competitors

  +
- Context
- Capabilities
- Channels
- Capital

  +
- Results

The first three C's are described earlier. The additional new elements add depth and utility to the model.

The *context* of a business describes the overall architecture of a market and its broad environment including regulatory structure, licensing regime, political influences, product/market combinations, technological environment, trade and quota arrangements, patent limitations, and other defining characteristics of the industrial environment.

Active management of these key elements of context is one of the biggest challenges in the creation of transnational business success. In some of the most dynamic and complex industries such as telecommunications, financial services and utilities, changes in the regulatory and other contextual elements are often a primary focus of senior management attention as they reshape the competitive landscape.

The *capabilities* of individuals and the organization are a critical source of incremental revenue, profits and competitive advantage in both manufacturing and service businesses. Much of strategy is about identifying, improving and employing as effectively as possible the human and competitive capabilities resident in a business.

Channels are the systems of distribution through which businesses deliver products and services to their customers and increase in strategic significance as businesses develop globally.

The ability to access, share, dominate, or even to own channels allows competitors to control the customer and restructure the value chain by reducing the time and cost involved in value delivery.

The ability to bypass intermediaries and go directly to the market, shortening the distance between producer and customer, creates enormous advantage over trailing competitors encumbered with older, less flexible channel structures and systems. This is the source of the success of the much praised Dell direct delivery model.

In addition, channels and customers are often tightly linked, with new channels providing access to new customers, as well as reducing costs and improving service to an existing client base.

Capital advantage and a strategic approach to the capital base and balance sheet of an organization is an often overlooked element of strategy. Too often strategy is focused exclusively on the internal operations, external market, cash flow and profit and loss account aspects of a business. No longer seen as merely sourcing funds at market prices, the effective management of corporate financial capital has become a major source of competitive advantage and creator of shareholder wealth.

Results, the final test of strategy, need to be specifically included to tie all elements of the model to a meaningful end.

In this 7C's + Results model there is an explicit linking of a strategy model with results, causing strategists to be constantly mindful of practicality, the need to implement ideas and the value of a process to assure that programs of strategy lead to action and the achievement of valuable goals.

Beyond the 7C's

Other C's that have cropped up for potential inclusion in the expanding ocean of "C" concepts include *Compensation*, *Core technologies*, *Communications*, *Compassion* and *Cooperation*. The application of these new C's can be considered for many businesses.

In order to get the best possible results, the application of the C of *Creativity* is worth considering at each and every part of the model.

Element 14: The "Rights" of Strategy

One of the greatest musical composers of all time, Igor Stravinsky, wrote a beautiful piece of music in 1913 entitled "The Rites of Spring", which captured the essence of birth and renewal of a new season.

Similarly, the "Rights" of Strategy can signal a fresh beginning for your own business. While developing your own strategy program, it is essential to ensure that your organization is fully in line with the seven "Rights" which can help you to navigate to a more successful strategic future.

- Right process
- Right attitude
- Right people
- Right content
- Right thought
- Right creativity
- Right results

1. Right Process

Thought through from beginning to end by a full team of contributors, including those responsible for the implementation effort.

2. Right Attitude

Open, honest, direct, as collaborative as possible and fully committed.

3. Right People

Ensuring that both definition and implementation of strategy are pursued to the highest quality and with the full commitment of the organization.

4. Right Content

Ensuring that all relevant issues and opportunities are raised and addressed.

5. Right Thought

Embracing a full understanding of the situation, competitive reality, customer views and real options, with no sacred cows or political obstacles standing in the way of progress.

6. Right Creativity

Thinking out of the box on both the process and content of strategy.

7. Right Results

Setting the right vision and objectives for the organization and using the strategy process as a best practice example of how to get things done.

These seven "Rights" need to be carefully monitored at all times. Although no checklist can replace the motivating effect of high quality leadership, respecting these rights and specifying the correlative responsibilities for all involved can support the achievement of the highest standards of excellence in your approach to strategy.

Part II. Principles of the New Paradigm

II.I Sharpening Your Focus

Element 15: Comparative Option Valuation

Strategy is about choices.

There will always be more options than any one company can pursue successfully. It is therefore essential to provide a coherent framework of option evaluation in order to select the most appropriate pathway forward.

The process of understanding, refinement, redefinition, evaluation and review of options should be as unconstrained and creative as possible. Getting this right will be one of the most significant steps in the history of your business.

- Value impact in capital markets
- Net present value
- Contribution to profitable growth potential
- Fit with organizational capabilities
- Impact on strategic balance sheet
- Positive change in customer relationships
- Contribution to competitive differentiation

1. Value Impact in Capital Markets

The impact of strategy, especially for listed companies, needs to be measured by the increase it is expected to create, or does create, in shareholder value.

This, in turn, is usually measured by the improvement in shareholder wealth as reflected in the equity market capitalization of the business, or in a total enterprise value calculation which adds together debt and equity values.

For privately owned companies, the improvement in debt ratings, implied enterprise value, or other standard can serve as a surrogate for an equity market value measure.

2. Net Present Value

An organization's net present value (NPV) is the discounted present value of all future cash flows, net of any initial cash investments. The NPV is the best measure by which to assess investments, make decisions, and track performance. The internal rate of return (IRR) may also be used for comparative purposes.

Maximizing NPV is the hallmark of any good operating management team. It underlies many of the approaches of fabled investor gurus such as Warren Buffett and many highly successful business owner-operators.

Perhaps the value of this cash flow-based measure is best captured in the statement that "Cash is King" in the business world.

3. Contribution to Profitable Growth Potential

Current value implications and the impact of immediate opportunities are not the only option valuation measures.

The potential to create future flows of revenue, profits, cash and value needs to be taken into consideration as well. This may be especially true in a high growth business, where enterprise value is driven by expectations of future growth in revenues and earnings.

As in tournament chess, good business strategists think many moves ahead.

4. Fit with Organizational Capabilities

As we have seen elsewhere, strategy is much about the ability of teams of individuals to design and execute predefined strategies, but it is also about preparing an organization to profit from unanticipated changes and developments in the business system.

An option which can enhance organizational capability should be valued more highly than one which does less to lift the future capabilities of the team involved.

5. Impact on Strategic Balance Sheet

The potential to upgrade the total set of assets and liabilities of a business—people, capability and strategic relationships as well as current and fixed assets—is another area for value creation which is difficult to assess mathematically, but can have a profound impact on long-term business success.

Addressing classic financial balance sheet categories and also taking into account the value of "soft", or non-traditional assets and liabilities, will ensure that all elements of value addition can be reviewed and accounted for.

6. Positive Change in Customer Relationships

Serving the customer is the *raison d'être* of any company.

The ability to drive those relationships to a higher level is an essential element in strategic assessment and valuation. This ability, taken partially into account by valuing both hard and soft assets and supported by taking a hard look at all variables of product, brand and service, cannot be forgotten in any strategic evaluation.

7. Contribution to Competitive Differentiation

Competitive differentiation in the areas that matter to customers and to your business system are a critical end point of successful strategy.

Although serving the customer better carries with it an implicit understanding of enhancing the competitive offer, it is important to assess directly the impact of your actions on truly differentiating performance in the market. Options which truly create "clear water" between a business and its rivals will create both immediate and future value.

Element 16: Setting Priorities

Setting priorities and deciding which initiatives will be pursued, and which will not, is one of the most important elements of strategy. Charting a clear path forward and allocating resources to achieve the objectives set along the way is both an art and a science.

The process described below sets out how a team can turn a list of good ideas into an effective set of priorities for action.

- Set the vision
- List potential actions
- Complete the priority matrix
- Select priorities
- Allocate resources
- Clarify the choices
- Implement the strategy

1. Set the Vision

Before setting out the list of potential strategic actions for a business it is necessary to agree what vision is being pursued.

Without a clearly stated overarching goal it is impossible to be sure that strategic priorities are going to align all aspects of a business in the correct direction. To ensure that rational choices are made the ultimate end goal of the enterprise needs to be understood by all participants.

2. List Potential Actions

Before imposing a framework to identify the priorities it is useful to ensure that you make a comprehensive list of all potential actions and opportunities.

It may also be useful to have a minimum threshold on the value of suggested actions. The actual cut-off level will depend upon the size and nature of the organization. The cut-off may be on initiatives which have a minimum potential annual impact on profit, NPV or market capitalization.

3. Complete the Priority Matrix

Each potential action on your list can now be placed on a 2 × 2 matrix to help decide upon priorities.

The matrix captures the value of each initiative, measured in either annual profit or longer term impact, along the horizontal axis. This requires the group to have a rough sense of the benefit and cost of each idea.

The vertical axis estimates how difficult it will be to implement each action.

Priority Matrix

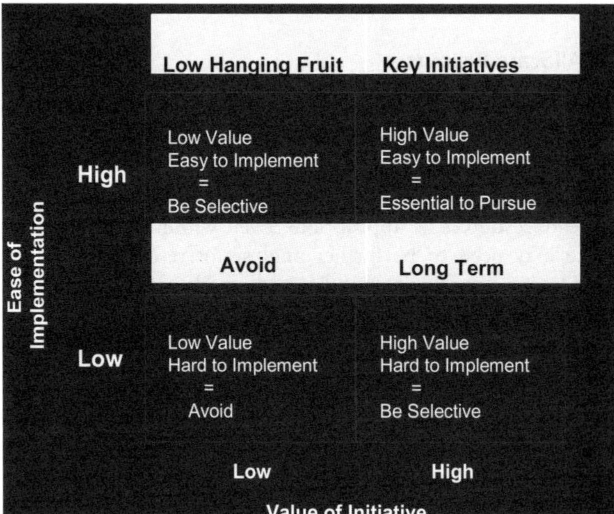

4. Select Priorities

The final phase of setting priorities requires you to decide how many of the proposed actions you can pursue well and which are better deferred or cancelled altogether.

Funds for investment may be limited, or there may be a limited management capacity for new programs due to the demands of running daily operations. Requirements or policies imposed by a parent company may also inhibit possible action.

These elements of limitation need to be considered individually and together to decide where to draw the line on the priority matrix.

Actions most likely to be pursued as priorities will fall within the high-value/easy-to-implement quadrant. All low-value/difficult-to-implement actions should be avoided.

The crunch quadrants are those which contain high-value/difficult-to-implement items and low-value/easy-to-implement items. In this instance, further analysis and discussion may be necessary to decide on the final priority selection.

In all cases, the priorities selected must be fully aligned with the overall vision and internally coherent as a set of actions.

5. Allocate Resources

Acting differentially and allocating resources in line with the agreed priority list are essential parts of the process of realizing full value from a prioritization exercise.

Having completed the matrix of priorities, managers can allocate resources as appropriate. Even within the priority list there may need to be further analysis of resources required, based upon a comparison of the needs and benefits of each item.

6. Clarify the Choices

Failure to differentiate in action between priority and non-priority items will significantly reduce the impact of your investments and the value of your overall strategic effort.

Perhaps the best way to lock in the value of your thinking is to set out on a separate three-column chart those initiatives which your organization will start, those which should be stopped and those which should be continued.

7. Implement the Strategy

This focus on priorities will enable you to exert the maximum force on the most powerful levers of change, avoid a diffusion of effort and maximize the impact of your choices on business profit and value during implementation of the strategy.

Element 17: SMARTER Goals

In order to achieve results it is important to have a set of goals or targets at which to aim and against which to measure progress. In the context of an effective strategy these goals need to be well crafted and fully understood by all involved.

The seven SMARTER characteristics of properly drafted goals are listed below. Ensuring that all goals and target results meet these criteria is well worth the effort. By turning these guidelines into actions the value and impact of your strategy is far more likely to be enhanced.

- Simple
- Meaningful
- Actionable
- Realistic
- Total
- Effective
- Results-driven

1. Simple

Complication can obscure clarity. Plain language, no jargon, short words and clear targets are necessary for goals to be understood.

2. Meaningful

Goals need to contribute to the achievement of the vision and strategy. Not all goals need to be pursued or highlighted. The goals stated should address priority targets, not list all potential objectives or activities.

3. Actionable

Statements of aspiration are difficult to set or measure as precise targets. Goals should be measurable, achievable and linked to concrete plans of action.

4. Realistic

Stretch goals can enhance the ability and achievements of an enterprise. Unrealistic goals, often imposed from above, may merely serve to discredit the strategy process and goal-setting exercise and demotivate the team involved.

5. Total

The set of goals promulgated and pursued must capture all facets of your strategy. Leaving out key parts can only result in inefficiency and increase the risks of strategic failure.

6. Effective

The goals, and the goal setting process, must be effective. They must support the overall strategy, be aligned with the overall mission of an enterprise and create sustainable competitive advantage.

7. Results-Driven

The goals set, and the rewards associated with their achievement, must reflect the value of achieving tangible results through strategy.

Process excellence is not a result, it is a means to an end. Real goals are often measured in improved revenues and profits, reduced unit or overhead costs, increases in market share, upgraded skills or capabilities, or other sources of tangible value and competitive advantage.

Element 18: Tactics

Good or bad tactics can determine the success or failure of a strategy. The most successful tactical approaches often involve significant preparation and activity before a broader strategic engagement is visible. Tactical activities can include gathering intelligence, analyzing information, positioning assets and individuals, signaling, negotiating, feinting, establishing alliances, completing anticipatory movements of resources, building capabilities and resources and pursuing all other initiatives to create strategic advantage against an adversary.

The best tactics are those which thoroughly prepare and build on the strongest capabilities of an organization. In some circumstances, the preparatory tactics can even obviate the need for a costly battle altogether. Sun Tzu captured the value of this kind of approach when he stated:

> *"... the best victories are from battles which have never been fought."*

By breaking down the conceptual content of tactics into a useable check-list of seven interrelated parts, strategists can be more thoughtful about the selection and execution of tactics on the ground to achieve their strategic goals.

- Objective
- Resources deployed
- Timing
- Sequence
- Degree of force applied
- Contingency
- Expectations

1. Objective

There must be a clear objective of the tactics deployed and alignment with the larger objective of the overall strategy.

2. Resources Deployed

The actual resources deployed need to be fully assessed and carefully allocated. This can include human resources, funds, assets and supporting infrastructure.

3. Timing

Timing is indeed of the essence. In setting out the timetable attention needs to be paid to both the internal and external factors determining an optimal time to launch an initiative. Competitive and customer considerations need to be weighed, along with assessments of organizational readiness and alternative demands on the resources to be deployed.

4. Sequence

No action is taken on a stand-alone basis. The sequence in which initiatives are undertaken, relative to moves made by colleagues, competitors and allies alike, can be critical. This sequence will need to consider the prior and succeeding steps in the overall plan of action.

5. Degree of Force Applied

There is always a range of force which can be applied in any situation by the resources deployed.

Determining the degree of force applied, or the magnitude of the move, will enable leadership to calibrate the expected impact of the initiative. A tactical burst of ad spending, for example, can be high or low in cost over a set time frame and relatively strong or weak in its effect.

6. Contingency

Unlike the view held by many academic theoreticians on the science of strategy, the set of tactics deployed in competition or combat must be flexible, in particular during a fierce competitive engagement or in the face of a military enemy. Soldiers and managers without a Plan B can be in unnecessary danger.

Contingency aspects of any sound tactical plan will need to be figured into the overall approach.

7. Expectations

Finally, there need to be clear expectations of the outcome.

In a war these expectations relate to casualties suffered, materiel lost, ground gained and psychological impact on the enemy. Actual results achieved against expectations can inform follow-up actions or trigger an all-out retreat. Setting expectations in advance is an essential part of both military strategy and tactics.

For some of the same reasons, the expectations of tactical deployment of business resources also need to be forecast. By setting out an expected outcome, the target results and broader consequences can be assessed in advance and appropriate actions taken. Follow-on actions can be reset and future tactics adjusted to reflect both the knowledge and the territory gained.

II.II Responsibility and Engagement

Element 19: Corporate Responsibility

By adopting a more enlightened attitude toward corporate responsibility and seeing it as a core element of strategy rather than as an isolated set of public relations activities, forward-thinking leaders can create opportunities to motivate staff, give a greater purpose to the enterprise and grow a network of beneficial relationships outside the walls of the corporation.

Since the era of truly responsible strategy is just dawning, there is much room still to innovate, experiment and create something new and special for the future which can, in turn, create benefits and avoid risks for all stakeholders in your enterprise.

There are seven key areas of corporate social responsibility for consideration by a management team. These areas encompass both internal (workplace, business system, reporting and governance) and external (customers, environment and community) elements.

- Workplace
- Business system
- Reporting
- Governance
- Customer rights
- Environment
- Community

1. Workplace

Ensuring that a company has as a clean, safe and fair working environment for employees is one of the most basic aspects of corporate responsibility.

Health and safety, lack of sexual, religious, or racial discrimination and other programs that will ensure a proper workplace are all necessary elements of a thoroughly designed modern strategy.

2. Business System

Responsibility can now extend beyond the borders of your own current business operations.

In a world where business processes are increasingly outsourced and relations between different organizations are becoming deeper and more complex, the notion of responsibility is being extended to all of those businesses which directly touch another. Partners, franchisees and other participants in a business system in breach of acceptable standards of responsibility can call into question the ethics and standards of all companies using their products or services.

Even customers can be subject to scrutiny. Private banks must ensure that clients do not bring to the bank any funds from criminal, money laundering or terrorist activities.

Suppliers as well as customers are scrutinized as the buyer's responsibility now extends back up the value chain. It is no longer acceptable to claim that a cosmetic product has not been tested on animals if suppliers to the ultimate manufacturer have been engaging in just such practices.

3. Reporting

Many of the recent corporate scandals dragging down the reputation of business as a whole are related to deceptive reporting, poor reporting procedures and lack of oversight.

Both the quality of reports and their content are increasingly being called into question. While FASB and similar global accounting standards bodies will continue to evolve the general standards and policies to be applied to corporate accounts, the quality of the data presented needs to be consistently accurate in each individual case.

Extended definitions of what should be reported, such as the triple bottom line initiative requiring companies to report on their environmental and community record along with their financial results, will continue to stretch the capabilities of accounting and control departments for some time to come.

4. Governance

Major policy recommendations by the Cadbury Committee in the United Kingdom and the Sarbanes-Oxley Act in the United States have called into question the most appropriate structure for senior management and the constitution of boards of directors. Whether welcome or not, increased scrutiny and reform are the order of the day in corporate governance around the world.

Transparency and independence from inappropriate influence come up regularly and will continue to be topical as business leaders design and populate board and committee memberships, outline board and committee procedures and establish information flows.

Higher quality standards also apply in the approach to chairmanship, the CEO role, succession planning and all other elements of corporate governance.

5. Customer Rights

Numerous consumer advocacy groups and sympathetic legislators have been slowly turning up the heat on the disclosure and service levels required by product and service providers. Information on product contents, packaging standards, return policies, product safety and other elements of burgeoning consumer rights all need to be fully understood and built into strategic plans as both risks and opportunities.

Already, greater corporate responsibility for the long-term effects of product use is emerging, even in product areas where sales are primarily to informed adult customers. This movement is led by legal actions against pharmaceutical companies, arms manufacturers, tobacco companies and alcoholic beverage providers.

Participants in industries seen to be contributing to an unhealthy lifestyle or dangerous activities will increasingly attract the attention and incur the costs of litigation from consumer advocacy groups capable of inflicting great economic or reputational damage on an individual company, or even an entire industry.

6. Environment

In no other area of business responsibility is there more attention being paid than to the various aspects of environmental regulation.

It is abundantly clear that there are a number of areas such as global warming, toxic waste management, industrial effluent treatment, pollution of air, water, and land, deforestation leading to land quality erosion and river silting, fish and mammal population depletion, loss of rainforest cover and a whole host of other environmental concerns, where blame is increasingly focused on the business community. In some areas, such as the response to global warming, the business community is already far more involved than governments have mandated, underscoring how important these societal issues are to the long-term interest of the broader business community.

Taking into account and responding properly to those areas of environmental responsibility which impact most directly on your business now has to be a key element within any comprehensive strategic plan.

7. Community

Contribution to, and participation in, projects within the local business community has always been good practice. The United Way Movement in the United States, and the many activities supported by MNCs in local communities in emerging markets, reflect the acknowledged benefit of being a good corporate citizen.

Element 20: Why Become Engaged?

There is a growing list of reasons why a more proactive approach to responsibility will be in the long-term best interest of all stakeholders in an enterprise. By understanding these reasons, particularly those relating to your own specific business issues, and acting on that knowledge, you can create economic benefit and reduce financial risk at relatively little cost.

For large, multinational enterprises in particular, the logic for a program of greater social responsibility may need to be clearly articulated and priorities adapted from a list of potential reasons for greater engagement.

- Legal systems
- Regulators and accounts
- Financial results
- Relative organizational capability
- Brand and business risk
- Team spirit and motivation
- Risk of backlash against business

1. Legal Systems

Demanding more responsible behavior from businesses is becoming a worldwide phenomenon. Some nations, and their legal systems, are leading this trend.

Already the United States has become the forum of choice for legal action against international players operating far from American shores. It is only a matter of time before US litigation brings more corporations from the US and beyond before American judges and juries to account for foreign activities and actions that are alleged to be detrimental to employees, suppliers, local communities, countries and the global environment.

2. Regulators and Accounts

With the clarifying potential of triple bottom-line accounting, which takes into account community and environmental impact as well as financial performance, companies can set out a broader and more engaging set of goals for their enterprise.

The Global Reporting Initiative, established in 1997, has begun to address many of the technical issues. Models of socially responsible accounting have already been tested at British Airways, the Body Shop, Shell, and TYU Empire at a practical operating level.

3. Financial Results

Ignoring a more critical public attitude toward business can be very expensive indeed.

Lost sales, loss of licenses to operate, increased litigation, fines, a greater tax burden and other direct and indirect economic costs can result from allowing businesses to continue to be negatively positioned or to act in an irresponsible manner. Both revenues and costs can move adversely through a failure to anticipate the flow of attitudes and events in this area.

4. Relative Organizational Capability

Strategies are often driven by younger individuals more motivated by personal engagement than outdated notions of paternalistic employment or relative compensation.

An enterprise with a greater sense of purpose and more laudable values, demonstrating sensitivity to personal lifestyle, community development and environmental impact will have a greater ability to attract, retain and motivate the best of a small pool of talented future leaders.

Managers of caring companies will therefore be serving shareholders well by encouraging those people who can really make a difference in the performance and value of a specific business enterprise.

5. Brand and Business Risk

In adopting a more activist stance toward responsible global corporate citizenship, caring companies will enhance the values of their branded products, as well as burnishing their overall corporate image. They will be better placed to build more enduring and therefore more valuable relations with their customers.

The Coca-Cola Corporation now lists maintaining its status as a leading responsible corporate global citizen as one of its six global priorities. Nokia has sponsored an entire advertising campaign communicating concerns over social issues. Benetton has long made edgy social and human issues a core focus of their advertising and brand. These initiatives are not only aimed at corporate image-building, but are also designed to impact positively on all corporate products and brands.

6. Team Spirit and Motivation

Perhaps the greatest challenge today in attracting, keeping, motivating and engaging employees is the need to create and communicate an overarching purpose of the organization.

By giving employees a broader sense of contribution and value, enlightened business leaders can discover a higher sense of purpose and inspire a greater level of performance, both individual and collective.

Engagement with worthwhile causes can make the workplace more a part of an individual's personal, even spiritual, fulfillment. Businesses are, on the whole, made up of good people with good values. Reaching into the deep sources of this motivating set of values will increase the pride, performance and value of almost any enterprise.

7. Risk of a Possible Backlash against Business

A general backlash against ever-larger businesses is far from impossible.

High profile international institutions and trade organizations have already been attacked, disrupted and besieged. This growing anti-business sentiment could be partially checked by visible actions to promote worthy causes and to place visible emphasis on business objectives that extend beyond maximizing the next quarter's earnings.

In part, this potential backlash is motivated by a misunderstanding of how businesses operate and how profitable they are. Even in the usually pro-business United States, according to a recent survey completed by Decision Quest/MCAA, three out of four males distrust US businesses. Average business margins are believed to be more than six times the average of eight percent.

With such a lack of understanding and smoldering resentment in one of the world's most commercial societies, one can only infer how volatile global anti-business sentiment must be and how little it would take to trigger an anti-big-business backlash in less welcoming and less wealthy nations.

Element 21: How the Private Sector Can Contribute

Enlightened leaders in the private sector can contribute in many ways to improve the state of the world in which they operate and benefit from that contribution.

Seven of the areas of greatest potential contribution can be transferred directly from the core skills of successful business.

- Strategic capability
- Implementation and organizational skills
- Political savvy and credibility
- Resources and distribution
- Mastery of technology
- Performance measures
- Entrepreneurial drive and leadership

1. Strategic Capability

Honed in the rough and tumble markets of free competition, the skills necessary to define and execute strategy are far more developed in the private sector than in most public sector institutions.

Winning businesses have an established strategic capability to set vision, clarify and police priorities, allocate resources, measure progress accurately and follow up as needed to ensure that the highest return possible is extracted from each investment or initiative.

The result is a culture and operating approach that is informed, meritocratic, rational, effective and efficient, ensuring that all available existing resources are mustered and well deployed.

2. Implementation and Organizational Skills

The business community values highly those executives who can create economic value through high quality strategy development and implementation.

Good implementation is almost always based upon a talent for structuring, staffing, directing and motivating a large or complex organization. Those skills and abilities would be highly valued in the societal area as well.

3. Political Savvy and Credibility

Global business is as much about process and politics as it is about substance. The same applies to the management of global affairs outside the commercial sphere.

In both worlds, the resolution of major challenges includes scarce resource allocation, managing governmental relations, the politics of large and numerous organizations and overseeing complex processes of change and transformation.

A large premium is now placed upon the effective communication of all aspects of problem, progress and solution. As a result, private sector expertise in the creation of media campaigns can support societal change as well.

Corporate philanthropists and respected business personalities can also bring extended credibility to initiatives for greater responsibility.

4. Resources and Distribution

Private sector businesses employ the majority of the world's working population and oversee the deployment of a great proportion of the world's capital resources. Within and across these pools of resource and capability, there is enormous potential to contribute to the implementation of global societal strategy.

Multinational corporations increasingly control the channels of global distribution and the flows of global information. Accessing these distribution systems is essential to many initiatives in education, health care, population control and environmental amelioration.

5. Mastery of Technology

Perhaps the greatest current gap between public and private sector capabilities lies in the application of technological resources.

This gap is visible whether one is looking at Internet exchanges of carbon and pollution units, the application of pharmaceutical products to reduce disease, or new supply chain logistics to transport food to areas of famine.

Technological advantage lies at the heart of many winning business strategies and could equally well contribute on a broader range of social strategies.

6. Performance Measures

Many efforts at social change flag because there is no meaningful scorecard of performance.

It is a long established truth in the commercial world that "what gets measured gets done." Even complex performance variables such as car dealership service levels or a broker's investment performance can be broken into components, weighted, evaluated and a single summary service score reported and acted upon. Importing such measurement discipline to areas of public concern would improve focus and increase the intensity of investment where it would be most valuable. A linking of results, culture and compensation practices would further enhance the value of a private-public sector alliance.

7. Entrepreneurial Drive and Leadership

Not all private sector activities with positive societal or environmental benefits need to be pursued on an unpaid *pro bono publico* basis. Reforestation, energy trading, pollution credit systems, water management equipment and other socially beneficial activities may also be developed on a for profit basis.

Such activities are not only likely to perpetuate beneficial activities, but are also able to increase the amount of energy dedicated to improving the overall state of affairs, since they make no claim on limited public and private sector "social" resources.

The spirit of enterprise and the profit motive can underpin many valuable societal initiatives. Recent initiatives to provide leadership in climate change, recycling and other issues show the potential for change when business leaders act in their longer-term self-interest.

Element 22: A Practical Approach

Broader notions of responsibility are not yet, for many companies, part of their core strategy. But times are changing fast. Responsibility, sustainability and engagement are now emerging as key elements of competition and differentiation for all types of businesses.

A businesslike and practical approach will magnify the impact of investments in programs of responsibility and increase the likelihood of their continuation into the future.

- Take a practical and clear approach
- Link to your core business
- Start where you are
- Organize effectively
- Set goals and achieve tangible results
- Communicate effectively
- Provide leadership

1. Take a Practical and Clear Approach

It may be more effective to apply social investments across a limited range of business-related activities than to fragment effort. Fragmentation may reduce the impact and the return on total corporate investment and imperil the continuity of the effort.

A shorter list, linked to a business system and organizational capabilities, may be a more practical approach.

Ensuring clarity of purpose will make a program more understandable and more motivating, promoting greater progress towards the goals of the programs selected and yielding a higher and faster payback on investment.

2. Link to your Core Business

It may be more effective and more valuable to select responsibility programs which are linked to the core skills, brands, products, services and strategic assets of your business. This will bring greater expertise to bear on specific challenges and improve results. Association with the effort is more easily communicated, remembered and understood. Impact can be greater since the created benefits are more closely linked to the participating enterprise.

A clean drinking water initiative, for example, may well make more sense for a beverage company than for a clothing company. An Indian poverty relief or educational program may make more sense for a multinational company operating in India than it does for a domestic US utility. Providing disposable syringes to impoverished African health care centers may be more the province of a medical products company than an engineering firm, which would be better placed to advise third world municipal authorities on sanitation and infrastructure.

3. Start Where You Are

Change starts more easily at home. Integrating the current strategic and operating objectives that a business pursues in its daily operations with the content of a broader societal agenda can have great impact. For example, addressing issues related to product safety, manufacturing effluent, employment practices or staff education can be a great starting place.

4. Organize Effectively

The results of a strategic societal program can vary as dramatically as those of commercial activities, and therefore the right organizational approach needs to be fully considered in both cases.

Although very much a part of modern business strategy, engagement in programs of corporate responsibility may still be seen by some as a distraction from core financial or operating objectives. Board and senior management involvement and endorsement may therefore be essential in advance of the launch of any initiative.

Building the most appropriate program of content needs to be—and needs to be *seen* to be—consistent with the long-term goals of the organization. Board understanding and support of a code of conduct or matrix of responsibility, perhaps even worked through a dedicated board committee on governance and responsibility, would be well advised.

5. Set Goals and Achieve Tangible Results

Consistent with applying the full disciplines of a business approach to corporate involvement in a program of broader engagement and responsibility, each individual initiative, each individual's involvement and each investment should have an associated set of targeted results. The same is true of the program as a whole.

The major weakness of most strategies, and of most strategic models, is their failure to lead to tangible results in the real world. By setting goals and targeting results early on, this weakness can be avoided. Even expensive investments can be fully justified by the results they create.

By monitoring progress against pre-set milestones, the program can be kept on track more easily with necessary small adjustments made earlier in the program's life.

6. Communicate Effectively

A significant part of the value created by a corporation's program of social responsibility will depend on an effective communication program.

Both internal and external constituencies need to be considered and a different approach crafted for each. Channels and message content need to be carefully selected and planned.

What needs to be communicated to whom, by whom and to what schedule needs to be determined and built into strategic, organizational and tactical discussions. Those decisions need to be developed and coordinated within an overall program of corporate activity and communication.

7. Provide Leadership

Consistent with the broader principles of leadership in a modern organization, the program of social responsibility should be led from the front and from the center. Visible, motivating leadership is essential. For the program to be successful, leadership must also operate behind the scenes, encouraging, adjusting, refocusing and ensuring that the strategies are well resourced and key tactics well executed.

In a networked organization, leadership does not always need to come from the most senior ranks. Often a younger generation of managers and colleagues can provide the best examples of effort, inspiration and personal dedication.

Passion, even more than position, can make for a good leader and role model in the effort to participate more fully in programs of societal improvement.

II.III Leadership and Organization

Element 23: Principles of Leadership

The exercise of leadership is one of the most important elements of strategy. By setting out a practical framework, leadership can be more thoughtful, can make more impact and can contribute greatly to the success of a chosen strategy.

- Empower the vision and the strategy
- Live the values
- Engage and motivate individuals
- Go beyond the conventional
- Lead from the front
- Lead from the center
- Get the job done

1. Empower the Vision and the Strategy

The process of empowerment of vision in a strategy program is not only about launching the effort. How you treat the process and content during and after the exercise may be even more critical to its success.

A large part of individual commitment to greater collective effort is driven by the single test of whether the path set by the leadership of a business is truly empowered across the entire organization. Not all existing activities will be in line with the new direction. Creating real change consistent with the vision and strategy is essential. One of the most inevitably visible aspects of empowering a new vision lies in articulating priorities and ensuring that they are respected.

While every individual can make a substantial contribution to the successful design and implementation of strategy, each and every individual within an organization is also a possible source of resistance, recalcitrance and inefficiency unless convinced of the direction set by the leadership team.

2. Live the Values (Demonstrate Character Through Action)

In accepting a leadership role there is also a responsibility incumbent upon leaders to live the values promulgated, provide a model for behavior which respects the corporation's value summary and demonstrate the higher values which provide the foundation and guiding ethical principles of an organization.

Among these ethical values there is none more important than personal integrity. Trust, faith, hope and many other higher aspects of human emotion are tied up in the complex psychological act of accepting leadership from another individual. Of all of the attributes of leadership, trust consistently emerges in research as the most valued by subordinates.

The balance of values desired from leaders reflects the fact that the true essence of leadership is much more about individual behavior and moral value than it is about possessing any particular skill or exhibiting any one personal style.

Personal integrity and mastery of the self are the ultimate sources of power in business and in life itself.

3. Engage and Motivate Individuals (Reach the Heart of Your Organization)

In every organization the vast majority of individuals want to do a good job, learn, grow as they work and contribute to the creation of something special. For many, there is a sense of unfulfilled promise and disengagement in what they do and a missing sense of a higher purpose in what they achieve.

By reaching the hearts as well as the minds and financial interests of your colleagues, by responding to their need to contribute to something greater than their individual selves, you will be able to release new levels of energy for performance and change in any business.

4. Go Beyond the Conventional (Set New Standards of Excellence)

No manager will ever achieve the more ambitious goals of strategy if he or she aspires only to be conventional in approach or average in result. None of the leaders who created great business success stories, from Henry Ford to Bill Gates, built a winning enterprise using someone else's blueprint.

While understanding that the past is always valuable, limiting oneself to that understanding is never the pathway to new standards of excellence and accomplishment. The essence of strategy lies in differentiation, in creativity and in the art and science of informed action to bring about change.

5. Lead From the Front (Master the Visible Aspect of Leadership)

The best business leaders are constantly mindful of the opportunities and risks inherent in the natural role of leadership from the front. Demonstrating clarity of vision and indicating collective direction is essential. Careful and effective communication is critical. Remaining positive is a valuable skill, even if it is personally taxing in many stressful situations.

Promulgating and policing priorities and policies is particularly important. Disciplining and correcting is necessary, but needs to be done selectively, carefully, constructively and almost always in private. Finding and demonstrating a sense of confidence, common purpose, and belief is invaluable. Any hint of hesitation, disbelief, or uncertainty, without a path to resolution, can be potentially confusing and costly to an entire organization.

6. Lead From the Center (Manage Formal and Informal Networks)

While mastering the skill of visible leadership from the front, leaders must also master the more subtle skill of leading from the center, or even from behind, guiding the group's progress with a less visible hand.

Modern leaders should take into consideration that technological and social evolution have combined to create a series of overlapping networks and informal communities within and across business borders, connecting businesses and influencing development in ways just beginning to be understood.

By mastering the art of the invisible hand, you can influence others to work together toward a desired outcome without overtly driving or dominating the process. You can create the results you want, along with a pride of ownership and sense of accomplishment in a team, that a more direct and interventionist approach from above may never be able to match.

7. Get the Job Done (Move Seamlessly From Understanding to Execution)

Simply put, many leaders fail because they just don't execute. Ensuring that you avoid this trap and get the job done, no matter how challenging the task, is the hallmark of an effective leader and a winning organization.

The best business leaders have much in common with star athletes. In addition to enormous pay packets, they are expected to lift the performance of an entire team and to outperform competition. Performance psychologists, drawing from their analysis of the best performing world-class athletes, have identified a single, dominant psychological variable between their subjects. Surprisingly, the characteristic was not a desire to win. The real motivator was a deep-seated fear of failure.

By refusing to accept failure, by getting the job done no matter how daunting the obstacles or how fearsome the adversary, is a true test of world-class business leadership.

Element 24: Strategic Organization

A strategic organization is an organization ready and fully equipped to undertake the challenges of successful strategy. As you prepare your own strategic process you will benefit from an awareness of the seven leading characteristics which allow an organization to maximize return from an investment in strategy.

- Sound operational platform
- Strategic framework
- Specific industry knowledge
- Strategic mind
- Conducive environment
- Conducive organization
- Receptive individuals

1. Sound Operational Platform

It is essential to have in place the basic business skills required to think and act strategically. A strategic organization will have the appropriate accounting, marketing, technological, analytical and organizational capabilities to operate and improve a business.

If these skills are not readily available, a specific program to develop or acquire them will be required.

2. Strategic Framework

A vision, while essential, cannot be developed in a vacuum. A thorough understanding of your business's past, present and future options is essential to create a single compelling vision going forward. In order to develop that vision and the supporting strategies within it, a clear framework to capture understanding and align action is needed. That overall framework, often a matrix with two relevant axes, will organize a comprehensive and useable set of inputs in a meaningful fashion. Such a matrix, for example capturing brand strength and distribution strength in a consumer goods business, can inform both strategic diagnosis and design.

3. Specific Industry Knowledge

It is essential to have a comprehensive understanding of current trends and dynamics within the context of your specific industry. This can include current and proposed competitive change, regulatory change, the impact of technological trends and global trends such as consolidation, which may be relevant for changing an existing approach.

It is interesting to note that disruptive technological changes—for example the onset of digital imaging in the photography industry—can usually be foreseen five to ten years in advance of their having a major impact on an industry or business.

Specific industry knowledge should always include an element of future thinking as well as past understanding. No one can navigate toward a successful strategic future using only a rearview mirror for guidance.

4. Strategic Mind

Having the right components available for strategic thinking is essential. Experience, capability, flexibility, creativity and schooled intuition are all essential for effective strategic process.

This is not just a question of willingness or attitude, but also of the fundamental capability to engage in the high level thinking required to design and implement good strategy.

5. Conducive Environment

It is impossible to design and implement strategies focused on realizing the full potential of an enterprise if that enterprise is riven by politics, saddled with a culture of blame and finger-pointing, or dominated by individuals attempting to assert their own agendas on others in a manner not fully aligned with the organization's best interests.

Only by ensuring that the work environment is open, honest and supportive can senior managers look forward to achieving good results from their strategic planning processes. Even if there is no wholesale change proposed in management structure, staffing, or operating principles, it is always important to address on a timely basis the counter-productive sources of irritation and resistance that can derail a strategy process and undermine efforts to achieve full operating potential. These sources may be found in inadequate data bases, overburdened IT or marketing staff, or even simple human character.

6. Conducive Organization

Even in an open, honest and supportive environment, it is important to have the appropriate organizational attention dedicated to the development and implementation of strategy. Order and discipline with regard to management time will be required to develop and implement strategies which can change the focus and priorities of operations and individual activities within a busy enterprise.

The process and content of strategy can only be fully realized in an organization whose structure, operating principles and priorities reflect the fundamental importance of strategy.

7. Receptive Individuals

All good strategies begin and end with individual effort. Strategy cannot be forced upon an organization unwilling to consider change.

Overt and covert resistance, recalcitrant individual behaviors and unwillingness to learn new skills and unlearn old patterns can all undermine or derail the best thought-out strategies.

By overcoming a natural resistance to change, individuals can become agents of change and leaders of strategy—to the benefit of themselves and their organizations. Getting the team right before you start the strategy process is an essential part of moving your business to a new level of excellence.

In his book *From Good to Great*, which analyzed the key success factors of a number of "good" performing companies which later became "great" success stories, Jim Collins discovered that the management team often had to change before the strategy and operations of a business could be fully tuned. Other experts have pointed out that in two-thirds of dramatically successful turnarounds, the old management team had to be replaced before significant progress could be made.

Element 25: Trends in Organizational Design

The past few years have seen seven accelerating trends that will affect the strategies—and therefore the organizations—of the new millennium. The summary results of those changes are organizations that are less expensive to operate, faster to respond to issues in the relevant markets, better at sharing data and ideas around a network. They reflect a greater use (and reliance) on technology to integrate activities and operations.

By assessing how well your own business is currently performing against each trend, opportunities may be surfaced which improve both business performance and business value.

- Global markets
- Acquisitions and mergers
- Strategic alliances
- More flexible and networked organization
- De-layering and downsizing
- A more technologically enabled paradigm
- Management of intellectual capital

1. Global Markets

One of the reasons that new forms of organization have emerged is that there has been a broadening of boundaries to embrace global and regional markets.

This change also brings in a longer list of competitors and a greater set of issues related to a business system. Organizations will need a specific strategy to respond to these challenges.

2. Acquisitions and Mergers

The second trend, related to the global consolidation phenomenon, recognizes the possible need to develop an acquisition, merger, or other "inorganic" growth program.

The biggest challenge in making mergers and acquisitions work lies in integrating two organizations successfully. It has long been known that, on average, mergers and acquisitions destroy shareholder value.

By preparing your organization to meet the challenges of post merger integration you will significantly improve the odds of a successful transaction should you decide to pursue this strategic pathway to growth.

3. Strategic Alliances

The third trend is to increase the number of strategic alliances, formal and informal, across borders and markets.

Failure rates in alliances are even higher than in mergers or acquisitions. Creating success against the odds will require greater skills and capabilities to manage relationships in complex hybrid organizations.

4. More Flexible and Networked Organization

The fourth trend is a move away from old-fashioned command and control structures and operating principles toward a more distributed and participative model of leadership and operation. A network organization may allow complex yet flexible strategies to be developed and executed effectively.

5. De-layering and Downsizing

The fifth trend is to reduce the number of organizational layers between top management and the customer. This often means reducing HQ staff dramatically and moving central resources back into divisions or directly into the field of operation.

It has long been understood that organizational learning takes place at the operating interface with the customer. More and more, organizations are setting themselves up to manage intellectual capital better and to harness the full value of the knowledge gained at that customer interface.

Another important challenge is to pursue a common global vision while serving local market needs.

Both these goals may demand a new organizational model as well as adaptations to company operating principles, values and strategies.

6. A More Technologically Enabled Paradigm

A sixth trend for consideration is the application of technology.

Software and hardware options need to be explored to see to what extent a smaller, more capable and better equipped team could improve both efficiency and effectiveness.

7. Management of Intellectual Capital

Finally, the increasing importance of actively managing intellectual capital will need to be taken into account when designing your organization.

Finding out where wisdom, information and skills reside in your organization, and how you draw on and profit from those valuable repositories, are critical elements in preparing your business for the future.

Element 26: Principles of the Orpheus Process

The award-winning Orpheus Orchestra is a large group of world class musicians playing the music of many of the world's greatest composers. Their performances are fresh and creative. They have captivated audiences in concert halls in every major capital city around the world.

Their exceptional capabilities come from a unique organizational approach which is based on a creative new model of self-leadership, with no conductor or visible leadership from any single person. Each member of the group contributes to the leadership and accomplishment of the overall result.

Not all orchestras or businesses are ready to move forward without a single leader to provide overall direction and specific instruction. Yet in applying the lessons learned from this fascinating Orpheus model there may well be opportunities to refresh your approach, to change the way you define and practice leadership and to reset the standards you seek to achieve in the creative elements of your own business strategy.

Making this model work requires the observation of seven unique principles.

- Leave your insecurities at home
- Communicate
- Know how and when to let go
- Understand "power with" and not "power over"
- Share in the leadership model
- Invest responsibility in others
- Admit we don't know everything

1. Leave your Insecurities at Home

Fragile egos are counter-productive. While ego is seen as important to give an individual the courage to put forward his or her own ideas to the group and to motivate individuals to achieve excellence in individual musical craftsmanship, the more sensitive side of performers' egos can stand in the way of a jointly-led organization.

2. Communicate

Even in a process which has a highly intuitive element, it is important to communicate effectively, including developing the skill of "active listening."

3. Know How and When to Let Go

Although the spirit of the Orpheus Process encourages all opinions to be heard, not all ideas can be adopted by the group. The process works at multiple levels to generate ideas on musical interpretation and performance and to weigh and select the ideas presented.

Members of the group who have originated ideas not adopted by the broader orchestra need to learn to move on, even if unhappy with the result. As one orchestra member put it bluntly: "You have to deal with rejection; it's part of the process."

4. Understand "Power With" not "Power Over"

Perhaps the neatest summary of the fundamental philosophy of Orpheus, the phrase "power with" captures the sentiment of shared empowerment and rejects the older notion of "power over", a characteristic of top down leadership.

5. Share in the Leadership Model

At the same time that there are extended rights under the distributed authority in Orpheus, there are also expanded responsibilities.

Everyone needs to participate to make the approach work. It was noted by members in the musical group that, while very participative, the group was not really open to any major shift in the basic model. Some of the most experienced Orpheus musicians who had been with the group since its founding pointed out that it would be very difficult to change a culture as strong and as essential to a group's functioning.

6. Invest Responsibility in others

The shared approach to leadership requires an ability to trust fellow musicians and the group as a whole.

The broader group is seen as a source of greater capability and wisdom than any one individual leader. The group is also seen as the source of a greater collective emotional intelligence which contributes to the creation of better musical performances.

7. Admit We Don't Know Everything

There is no room for a sense of infallibility in either the individual or the group in the Orpheus Process.

The group and its presentations are constantly evolving through challenge, renewal and change. An admission that all is never known keeps the group fresh, open to new ideas and ensures that there is always room in the future for constructive change.

Element 27: Testing Organizational Design

Good strategy is not just about respecting principles and directives. Asking the right questions is an equally important part of the process.

By responding to seven standard questions which can be used to test the quality and effectiveness of all types of organization, fresh and creative thinking can also be well anchored in the traditional disciplines of human capital management.

At each stage of proposed organizational change these basic questions need to be asked to ensure that the organization is prepared and structured to ensure that your strategies are fully and properly implemented.

- Minimal layers between management and customers?
- Reasonable spans of control?
- Right quality of people in place?
- Job descriptions clear?
- Potential conflicts eliminated?
- Rewards fully in line?
- Likely problems surfaced and addressed?

1. Minimal Layers between Management and Customers?

Many CEO's, even of some of the world's largest corporations, are constantly revising their organizational plans to minimize the number of layers between senior management and customers.

Past models, some with ten or more layers between senior management and customers, have proven to stifle constructive interactions and result in poor quality decision-making.

2. Reasonable Spans of Control?

At the same time that excessive layers can reduce the quality of decision-making and inhibit the value of mandated action, excessively wide spans of control can be equally inappropriate.

Too many direct reports can also dilute the value of information flow upward and reduce the quality of input from managers to those reporting to them.

3. Right Quality of People in Place?

All critical views of strategy and of strategic success confirm that changing or moving people is often an essential part of strategy.

The first two questions above address the structure of an organization. This question requires managers to assess the quality and appropriateness of individuals in relation to their position within the organization—and change or move them if necessary.

4. Job Descriptions Clear?

Once the right people are in place, it is essential that their responsibilities are fully understood by all. A full and accurate job description, against which carefully structured performance reviews can be made, can ensure that each member of an organization is both efficient and effective.

5. Potential Conflicts Eliminated?

Even allowing for the production of full and accurate job descriptions, shared responsibilities and some blurring of borders is inevitable.

Participation on task forces, joint deliverables and team effort can lead to better results or to dysfunctional conflict if not properly managed.

All sources of potential conflict need to be addressed and eliminated to ensure the smooth functioning and long term success of an organization.

6. Rewards Fully in Line?

The systems of reward, recognition, promotion, hiring, firing and job allocation all need to be fully supportive of the new directions of your strategy.

Just as one misaligned element in the content of strategy or setting of organizational goals can reverberate negatively across many aspects of a business system. A reward system in particular which does not align fully with the strategic goals set for a business can create disharmony and inefficiency on a significant scale.

7. Likely Problems Surfaced and Addressed?

In addition to the potential for conflict at the structural level identified above, it is often useful to ask the question: Are there any other aspect of the organization—role of directors, intervention by owners, missing functions, overburdened departments, changes in IT, or other—which could have a negative impact on the successful implementation of strategy?

All relevant issues which surface as a result of this question should be addressed as early as possible.

The Final Element: Beginning Your Own Strategy

We end with a beginning.

Having read through the full content of this book and having adapted each insight to fit your own set of business challenges, you are now fully equipped to embark on, or to amend, your own strategy program.

- Assemble and brief core team
- Outline timetable
- List participants in the process
- Develop a communications program
- Allocate responsibilities
- Specify meeting schedule
- Emphasize results

A set of immediate next steps is set out below to ensure that momentum is not lost and actions leading to results can begin.

1. Assemble and Brief the Core Team

The core strategy team is usually made up of between three and eight individuals who will oversee the strategic planning program from beginning to end.

In most cases the team is led by the Chief Executive. The Finance Director, Strategic Planning Director or Marketing Director may also take the lead role for strategy development.

The strategy will probably need to be signed off by the Chairman, members of the board of directors, or the proprietors in a non-publicly quoted business. Their inclusion in the process needs to be carefully considered, as each decision maker or influencer needs to be given adequate time to digest the material and contribute to the process.

2. Outline an Overall Timetable

Start dates and dates of delivery need to be set.

Usually, the three stages which make up a strategy program—diagnosis, design, and implementation planning—will require different time periods.

Assuming a twelve-week period for the total exercise, the diagnostic phase may take four to six weeks, the design phase may take four weeks; and the implementation planning phase may take a final two to four weeks, during which the program can be drafted and approved by all parties.

The elaboration of a full tactical plan or supporting detailed plans in HR, operations, or other areas may take much longer. To some extent size and complexity matters. A strategic program in a large and complex multi-business organization can take much longer than a similar plan in a smaller and more focused company.

Obviously, the actual implementation process will take much longer to complete than the three preparatory phases. Programs of cultural change can take years to implement fully. Integrating a significant acquisition, particularly if for the first-time, may be at least a two-year process.

3. List Participants in the Process

This list will include the core team which will provide the majority of supervisory effort required to complete the strategy, the support team who will leverage the time of their senior colleagues and those individuals who will make defined contributions to specific parts of the plan. This can be quite a long list and may need to be put together in stages.

Getting the right stars involved may be far more important than assembling a cast of thousands to support the effort. In fact, experience shows that a central or supporting group which is too large can actually be counter-productive.

Too many people around the table can create a diffusion of effort, can extend meeting times without adding value and can delay the accomplishment of work objectives by leading to too broad an involvement in a narrowly focused set of activities. On the other hand, enlisting a few of the very best in an organization will speed results and serve as a clear signal of the importance and expected value of the effort.

4. Develop a Communications Program

An internal communications program should be developed to brief key constituencies on the strategy exercise.

This briefing will be necessary in order to instill a broad-based sense of ownership in the process, as not everyone can be involved in the detailed activity of designing the strategy and drafting the strategic documentation.

Beyond those who will contribute specific input into the strategy is a larger group who will need to be informed of progress, provide interpretation for the working team on selected areas of data and propose any creative ideas on the ultimate direction of the strategy.

This wider group may work informally via email, or can be assembled at critical points in the strategy program to discuss the data, its interpretation, the range of options and provide guidance on the shaping of the strategy going forward.

5. Allocate Responsibilities

Once the team members have been selected and the communications program started, the precise responsibilities of each team and team member need to be allocated.

There should be no slippage or room for misunderstanding around deliverables and the dates for delivery. Where relevant, responsibilities should include sign off on content from other parties to the process. A marketing department's analysis of customer profitability, for example, should require the input and consent of the finance, audit, or control team.

Properly allocated responsibilities address content, process and timing on an integrated basis. Each member of the team, from CEO downward, should have a clear statement of his or her role, his or her responsibilities, and the key tasks for which he or she is responsible.

6. Specify Meeting Schedule

Following agreement on an overall timetable, team membership and allocation of responsibilities, a meeting schedule should be set which ties in to the specified responsibilities and dates of delivery.

Ideally, the meeting schedule should take advantage of opportunities when teams or individuals from remote geographies are already assembled, thus reducing travel expenses and maximizing man-hour efficiency.

In developing this schedule, many experienced companies will incorporate off-site strategy sessions. These sessions, which can last from one to three days, take people out of the ordinary working environment and existing mind-set, benefiting from a different meeting place where fresh ideas and creative thought processes can emerge more easily.

7. Emphasize Results

Because the demands of modern strategy are often different from past approaches and expectations for better results will be high, a results-driven approach should be "hardwired" into the program from the very first agenda.

Target results should be incorporated into operating plans, built into budgets, integrated into management objectives and reflected in performance reviews and compensation. The appropriate organizational structure and individual commitments also need to be aligned, as do systems of operating, financial and strategic control.

The core message that the most important output of strategy is the achievement of results needs to be constantly repeated throughout your program.

By beginning with a statement of the end results desired, strategic leaders can set out with a higher likelihood of success.

Epilogue

Strategy is, according to the definition set out at the beginning of this book, the art and science of informed action. Mere theory is never enough.

The test of any strategy will be measured by the achievement of measurably better results and the creation of tangible value in a real business environment.

Strategy is not an easy process. It cannot be completed quickly or superficially if world class results are expected. There is no substitute for thoughtful, conscientious completion of each step in the process.

Every journey of a thousand miles begins with a single step. By taking that first step, your own inexorable flow from logic to action can begin.

I wish you well in your endeavors.